AAT

Personal Tax FA 2020

Level 4
Professional Diploma in
Accounting
Course Book
For assessments to
June 2023

Fifth edition 2020

ISBN 9781 5097 3405 4
ISBN (for internal use only) 9781 5097 3404 7

British Library Cataloguing-in-Publication Data
A catalogue record for this book is available from the British Library

Published by

BPP Learning Media Ltd
BPP House, Aldine Place
142-144 Uxbridge Road
London W12 8AA

www.bpp.com/learningmedia

Printed in the United Kingdom

Your learning materials, published by BPP Learning Media Ltd, are printed on paper obtained from traceable sustainable sources.

Contents

Introduction to the course

Syllabus overview

This unit is about the key aspects of taxation that affect UK taxpayers. It covers income tax, National Insurance (NI), capital gains tax and inheritance tax.

This unit provides students with the underpinning theory on taxation, such as what makes for a fair and equitable taxation system. Students then explore three core areas of income that contribute to a taxpayer's income tax liability: employment income, income from investments and income from property. Deductions and reliefs that apply to this income are then covered, so that students can compute the net income tax payable or reclaimable for a UK taxpayer.

The unit covers NI as applicable to employment income, together with the key principles that are part of capital gains tax and inheritance tax.

Students are also expected to demonstrate their knowledge and understanding of how UK taxpayers can minimise their tax liability legally. For example, someone with interest income larger than the savings income nil rate band investing in an individual savings account (ISA) will ensure that interest will be exempt from tax, whereas the same income from a building society will usually give rise to a tax implication. The ethical issues that surround this complex area will also be considered.

Taking all areas together, students will gain knowledge and understanding of all key areas of UK tax that can affect an individual UK taxpayer.

Personal Tax is an optional unit.

Test specification for this unit assessment

Assessment method	Marking type	Duration of assessment
Computer-based assessment	Partially computer/ partially human marked	2.5 hours

	Learning outcomes	Weighting
1	Analyse the theories, principles and rules that underpin taxation systems	10%
2	Calculate a UK taxpayer's total income	28%
3	Calculate income tax and National Insurance (NI) contributions payable by a UK taxpayer	23%
4	Account for capital gains tax	27%
5	Discuss the basics of inheritance tax	12%

Assessment structure

2.5 hours duration

Competency is 70%

A significant amount of tax information is provided to you in the assessment. This is reproduced in this book in the *Reference material and tax tables* section.

The guidance available about the assessment structure is based on the two sample assessments available on the AAT website. These two assessments both follow the same structure (outlined in the table below), and under previous syllabi the live assessment always followed the same structure as the relevant AAT sample assessment for that syllabus.

*Note that this is only a guideline as to what might come up. The format and content of each task may vary from what we have listed below.

The sample assessments both consisted of 13 tasks.

Task	Content	Max marks	Chapter ref	Study complete
Task 1	**Professional conduct – ethics** Written task, human marked	10	10 The tax and ethical framework	
Task 2	**Benefits in kind** Calculation of car and fuel benefits	8	3 Employment income	
Task 3	**Benefits in kind** Calculation of other benefits	8	3 Employment income	
Task 4	**Investment income** Calculation of taxable investment income from interest and dividends and the tax thereon including exempt income	6	1 Taxable income	
Task 5	**Property income** Calculation of taxable rental income and allowable expenditure for a number of different properties	6	4 Property income	

Task	Content	Max marks	Chapter ref	Study complete
Task 6	**Computation of taxable income and tax thereon** Assessed via free text box and human marked in live assessment. Requirement to list out net income, deduct personal allowance and calculate tax	12	1 Taxable income 2 Calculation of income tax	
Task 7	**National Insurance** Calculation of National Insurance Contributions	4	5 National insurance	
Task 8	**Sundry issues** This tested a number of separate areas: • Exempt income • Benefits • Tax planning • Personal pension contributions	7	3 Employment income 1 Taxable income 2 Calculation of income tax	
Task 9	**Basics of capital gains tax** This task required calculations for a number of different disposals testing chattels rules, connected parties, private residence relief, exempt assets and part disposals	10	6 Chargeable gains 8 Private Residence relief	
Task 10	**Taxation of share disposal** Assessed by free text box and human marked. Rights and bonus issues were tested.	10	7 Share disposals	
Task 11	**Capital gains tax payable** Question required calculation of capital gains tax payable for a number of taxpayers with different income levels. Also, dealing with capital losses	7	6 Chargeable gains	

Task	Content	Max marks	Chapter ref	Study complete
Task 12	**Inheritance tax** Multipart question testing several inheritance tax rules	6	9 Inheritance tax	
Task 13	**Inheritance tax** Detailed death tax on lifetime gifts and death estate calculation. Assessed by free text area and human marked	6	9 Inheritance tax	

Skills bank

Our experience of preparing students for this type of assessment suggests that to obtain competency, you will need to develop a number of key skills.

What do I need to know to do well in the assessment?

This unit is one of the optional Level 4 units. To be successful in the assessment you need to be able to:

- Calculate employment income including benefits in kind

- Calculate property income

- Produce a schedule showing income from all sources including investment income

- Calculate the personal allowance a taxpayer is entitled to

- Calculate income tax and national insurance for a wide range of taxpayers including those who have given money to charity or paid into a pension

- Calculate the chargeable gains arising in different scenarios including the disposal of shares and private residences

- Calculate inheritance tax

Assumed knowledge

No prior knowledge of tax is expected but if you have worked in tax or previously studied the *Business Tax* unit then you will have an immediate advantage.

Assessment style

In the assessment you will complete tasks by:

1   Entering narrative by selecting from drop down menus of narrative options known as **picklists**

2   Using **drag and drop** menus to enter narrative

3   Typing in numbers, known as **gapfill** entry

4   Entering **ticks**

5   Entering **dates** by selecting from a calendar

6   Writing written explanations in a very basic word processing environment which has limited editing and no spelling or grammar checking functionality

7   Entering detailed calculations in a very basic spreadsheet environment that has limited editing functionality and will not perform calculations for you

You must familiarise yourself with the style of the online questions and the AAT software before taking the assessment. As part of your revision, login to the **AAT website** and attempt their **online practice assessments**.

Answering written questions

In your assessment there will be a written question on ethics. The main verbs used for these type of question requirements are as follows, along with their meaning:

- Identify – analyse and select for presentation
- Explain – set out in detail the meaning of
- Discuss – by argument, discuss the pros and cons

Analysing the scenario

Before answering the question set, you need to carefully review the scenario given in order to consider what questions need to be answered, and what needs to be discussed. A simple framework that could be used to answer the question is as follows:

- Point – make the point
- Evidence – use information from the scenario as evidence
- Explain – explain why the evidence links to the point

For example if an assessment task asked us to explain which three of the fundamental ethical principles are most threatened in the following situation:

You are working on a company's corporation tax return, and notice some errors in the previous year's return which has already been filed. Your manager is concerned about the implications for their own career if the errors are disclosed, and has said that you would be considered for promotion if you agreed to keep quiet about the errors.

We could answer as follows:

1   Point – state which principles are most threatened – objectivity, integrity, professional behaviour

2   Evidence – use information from the scenario – the manager is asking me to keep quiet about an error and offered to consider me for promotion if I keep quiet

3   Explain – explain why the evidence links to the point – the manager is trying to influence my behaviour (objectivity), the manager wants me to act in a way that is not straightforward and honest (integrity), the manager wants me to behave in a way that is not legal and may discredit the profession (professional behaviour)

Introduction to the assessment

The question practice you do will prepare you for the format of tasks you will see in the *Personal Tax* assessment. It is also useful to familiarise yourself with the introductory information you **may** be given at the start of the assessment.

You have **2 hours and 30 minutes** to complete this sample assessment.

This assessment contains **13 tasks** and you should attempt to complete every task. Each task is independent. You will not need to refer to your answers in previous tasks. Read every task carefully to make sure you understand what is required.

Task 1 requires extended writing as part of your response to the question. You should make sure you allow adequate time to complete this task.

Where the date is relevant, it is given in the task data.

You may use minus signs or brackets to indicate negative numbers **unless** task instructions say otherwise.

You must use a full stop to indicate a decimal point. For example, write 100.57 NOT 100,57 or 100 57.

You may use a comma to indicate a number in the thousands, but you don't have to. For example, 10000 and 10,000 are both acceptable.

If rounding is required, normal mathematical rounding rules should be applied **unless** task instructions say otherwise.

---

1   As you revise, use the **BPP Passcards** to consolidate your knowledge. They are a pocket-sized revision tool, perfect for packing in that last-minute revision.

2   Attempt as many tasks as possible in the **Question Bank**. There are plenty of assessment-style tasks which are excellent preparation for the real assessment.

3   Always **check** through your own answers as you will in the real assessment, before looking at the solutions in the back of the Question Bank.

Key to icons

Key term

Key term

A key definition which is important to be aware of for the assessment

Formula to learn

A formula you will need to learn as it will not be provided in the assessment

Formula provided

A formula which is provided within the assessment and generally available as a pop-up on screen

Activity

An example which allows you to apply your knowledge to the technique covered in the Course Book. The solution is provided at the end of the chapter

Illustration

A worked example which can be used to review and see how an assessment question could be answered

Assessment focus point

A high-priority point for the assessment

Open book reference

Where use of an open book will be allowed for the assessment

Real life examples

A practical real life scenario

AAT qualifications

The material in this book may support the following AAT qualifications:

AAT Professional Diploma in Accounting Level 4, AAT Professional Diploma in Accounting at SCQF Level 8.

Supplements

From time to time we may need to publish supplementary materials to one of our titles. This can be for a variety of reasons, from a small change in the AAT unit guidance to new legislation coming into effect between editions.

You should check our supplements page regularly for anything that may affect your learning materials. All supplements are available free of charge on our supplements page on our website at:

www.bpp.com/learning-media/about/students

Improving material and removing errors

There is a constant need to update and enhance our study materials in line with both regulatory changes and new insights into the assessments.

From our team of authors BPP appoints a subject expert to update and improve these materials for each new edition.

Their updated draft is subsequently technically checked by another author and from time to time non-technically checked by a proof reader.

We are very keen to remove as many numerical errors and narrative typos as we can but given the volume of detailed information being changed in a short space of time we know that a few errors will sometimes get through our net.

We apologise in advance for any inconvenience that an error might cause. We continue to look for new ways to improve these study materials and would welcome your suggestions. If you have any comments about this book, please use the review form at the back.

These learning materials are based on the qualification specification released by the AAT in May 2020.

Taxable income

1

Learning outcomes

2	Calculate a UK taxpayer's total income
2.2	**Calculate income from investments** • Personal savings allowance • Identify and calculate taxable investment income • Identify exempt investment income
3	**Calculate income tax and National Insurance (NI) contributions payable by a UK taxpayer**
3.1	**Calculate personal allowances** • Calculate personal allowances • Calculate restrictions on personal allowances
3.2	**Apply relief for pension payments and charitable donations** • Apply private pension schemes • Apply charitable donations
3.5	**Advise on tax planning techniques to minimise tax liabilities** • Maximise relevant exemptions and reliefs • Change investment incomes to make them more tax efficient • Make other changes that can minimise tax liabilities

Assessment context

Calculating taxable income is a step on the way to calculating income tax payable which we will consider in Chapter 2. In the initial AAT sample assessment Task 4 tested the rules on investment income seen in this chapter and Chapter 2 for 6 marks. Task 6 required you to perform a detailed income tax calculation using the rules in this chapter and Chapter 2. It also required you to do a separate personal allowance restriction working. 12 marks were available in total. Task 8 consisted of a number of requirements for 7 marks, one of which tested tax planning for a couple with investment income, another tested the tax planning technique of paying into a personal pension scheme to reduce net income and thus preserve the personal allowance.

Qualification context

If you are studying *Business Tax* as well as *Personal Tax* then the material in this chapter will be useful background for you in your *Business Tax* studies. However, you will not be tested on the material in this chapter in the *Business Tax* CBT.

Business context

Preparation of taxable income computations forms part of the work a tax adviser will perform for their client.

Chapter overview

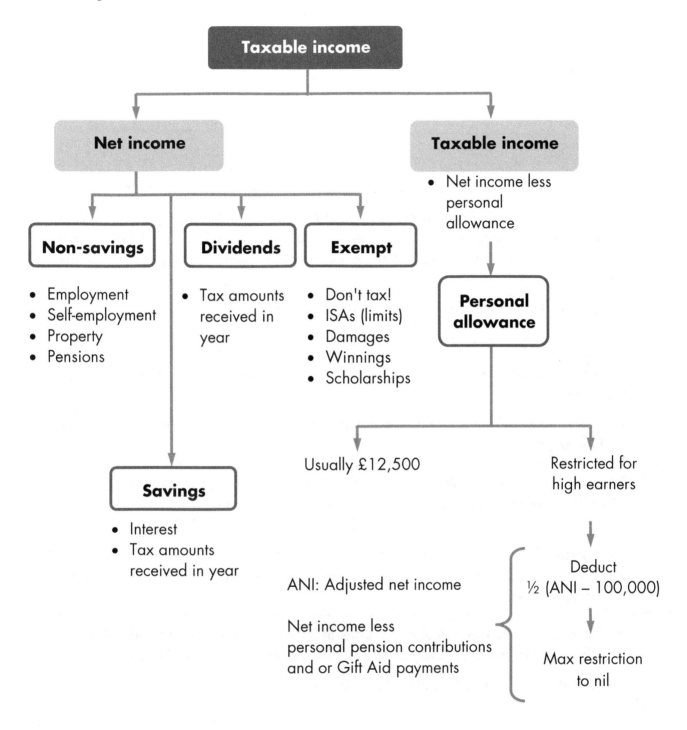

Introduction

In this first chapter we are going to look at the income tax computation and discover what makes up **taxable income**. An individual may have income from a number of sources, for example from employment, or from investments such as savings or property. We need to identify which of these are taxable, and then add them all together to get our **total or net income**, the amount that we will potentially have to pay tax on.

We'll find out how to calculate the actual employment and property income figures themselves in later chapters, for now we'll focus on **savings and dividend income**. We'll also identify some **exempt** income that will never be taxed.

Most taxpayers are given a **personal allowance**, an amount they are allowed to earn before they pay tax. We will deduct this personal allowance from the net income to leave us with our **taxable income**, the amount we will actually pay tax on.

We'll consider the actual calculation of tax in Chapter 2.

1 The income tax computation

The **income tax computation** is used to calculate an individual's **income tax liability**.

The income tax liability is the total amount of income tax the taxpayer is due to pay for the tax year.

Key term

Taxable income To calculate the income tax liability we apply tax rates to **taxable income**. Taxable income is the grand total of a taxpayer's income from all sources after deducting the **personal allowance**, if applicable.

Personal allowance The personal allowance is the amount of income a taxpayer is allowed to earn before they pay tax. It can be reduced or withdrawn completely for higher earners.

In this chapter we will calculate taxable income. We will then consider how to calculate the income tax liability on the taxable income in the next chapter.

The calculation of taxable income looks like this:

Assessment focus point

Proforma income tax computation

	Non-savings income £	Savings income (excluding dividends) £	Dividends £	Total £
Employment income	X			X
Property income	X			X
Interest received		X		X
Dividends from UK companies			X	X
Total/net income	X	X	X	X
Less personal allowance	(X)			(X)
Taxable income	X	X	X	X

Note. Total and net income are actually two different concepts but in your syllabus the terms can be used interchangeably. We will use net income for the rest of the chapter.

You will see there are three columns representing three types of income. We will consider the implications of this in the following section.

Some income will be paid over to the taxpayer **net of tax**, meaning tax has already been deducted at source. An example of this would be a salary payment from an employer. This represents an estimate of the tax the taxpayer is likely to have to pay.

We use the income tax computation to calculate the correct amount of tax that a taxpayer should be paying for the year. We therefore need to include all income **gross** of tax, before these estimated amounts of tax have been deducted.

When the tax liability has been calculated then the individual is allowed to deduct the tax already paid for the tax year. This may or may not be the correct amount.

This could leave the taxpayer having to make an additional tax payment or claim a tax repayment.

2 Non-savings, savings, dividend and exempt income

Different tax rates apply to the three different types of income:

Key term

Non-savings income This consists of income from employment, self-employment, pensions and property income.

Savings income This consists of interest received in the tax year.

Dividend income This consists of dividends received in the tax year.

Note. that exempt income is income that is never charged to income tax.

2.1 Non-savings income

This is all income other than interest and dividends. It includes the following:

- Income from employment (see Chapter 3 Employment Income)

- Income from property (see Chapter 4 Property Income)

- Income from pensions

- Income from self-employment (the calculation of this income forms part of the *Business Tax* syllabus)

2.2 Savings income

This is interest received. Note it is taxed on an actual basis. If interest is received in the tax year it is taxed. If it is accrued but not received, it is not taxed.

We simply add together all the interest received in the tax year from all sources and then insert the total into the savings column in the tax computation.

Most taxpayers will not have to pay income tax on interest received unless their interest income is above the **personal savings allowance** (see following chapter).

Illustration 1: Savings income

Gerry receives the following interest:

	£
Lloyds Bank	80
Nationwide Building Society	400
Government interest (gilts)	100

These amounts would be added together to calculate the total interest to be included in the savings column of the tax computation.

	Gross £
Lloyds Bank	80
Nationwide Building Society	400
Government interest (gilts)	100
Total	580

2.3 Dividend income

Taxpayers are taxed on the amount of dividend received in a tax year.

Illustration 2: Dividend income

Maria receives a dividend of £900. This is the gross amount that needs to be included in the computation of net income.

Most taxpayers will not have to pay income tax on dividend received unless their dividend income is above the **dividend allowance** (see following chapter).

2.4 Exempt income

Assessment focus point

Certain income is exempt from income tax. Do not include it in your total of taxable income.

If you are typing in an answer and there is exempt income in the question, state that this is exempt or if there is an exempt box to click, make sure you do this – there will be a mark here.

Exempt income includes the following:

2.4.1 Individual savings accounts (ISAs)

(a) These are special savings accounts a taxpayer can invest in.

(b) Individuals may invest up to £20,000 in an individual savings account (ISA) in tax year 2020/21. This could be in the form of cash, shares, unit trusts or insurance policies. Investors may use their entire allowance on one type of investment (eg the whole £20,000 could be invested in cash) or a combination of different investments.

(c) Dividend income from shares and interest income received from cash invested in an ISA are free of income tax. Capital growth is also free of capital gains tax.

(d) An ISA may be opened by someone 16 years old and over if it only contains cash.

(e) ISAs containing investments other than cash may only be opened by someone at least 18 years old.

2.4.2 Others

- Damages awarded as a result of personal injury or death and interest thereon

- Scholarships/grants, if paid to a student; taxable if paid to their parent as part of their employment income

- Prizes, lotto winnings, gambling winnings

- Premium bond prizes

Activity 1: Taxable and exempt income

Foster receives the following income:

	£
Building society interest	40
Dividend from an ISA investment	900
Rent	6,000
Non-ISA dividends	450

Required

Complete the following table.

Use the picklist options to list the sources of income under the appropriate headings (exempt, non-savings, savings or dividend income).

Record the amounts received under the appropriate column heading (exempt, non-savings, savings and dividends).

You do not need to total the columns.

Solution

Exempt income	Exempt income £	Non-savings income £	Savings income £	Dividend income £
Non-savings income				
Savings income				
Dividend income				

Picklist:

Building society interest
ISA dividend
Non-ISA dividend
Rent

3 Computation of taxable income

We will now revisit the full income tax computation we looked at in Section 1.

3.1 Net income

In a tax year, all income must be brought together and totalled.

The income is split into three columns representing the three types of income subject to tax:

- Non-savings income
- Savings income
- Dividend income

This gives us net income.

3.2 Taxable income

The personal allowance of £12,500 is then usually deducted from the total/net income to give the taxable amount.

The personal allowance is initially available to all taxpayers, including children.

The personal allowance is reduced for taxpayers who have income in excess of £100,000. The allowance can be potentially reduced to nil.

It is usually most beneficial to deduct the personal allowance against non-savings income before savings income then dividend income.

Illustration 3: Taxable income

In 2020/21, Joe has trade profits of £3,000 and receives bank interest of £17,500 and dividends of £500. Joe's taxable income for 2020/21 is:

	Non-savings income £	Savings income £	Dividends income £	Total £
Trade profits	3,000			3,000
Bank interest		17,500		17,500
Dividends			500	500
Net income	3,000	17,500	500	21,000
Less personal allowance	(3,000)	(9,500)	–	(12,500)
Taxable income	–	8,000	500	8,500

Activity 2: Taxable income

Quentin earns a salary of £3,000 in 2020/21. He receives rental income of £1,000, building society interest of £3,750 and a dividend of £5,000.

Required

Prepare a computation of taxable income for 2020/21, clearly showing the distinction between the different types of income.

Solution

	Non-savings income £	Savings income £	Dividend income £	Total £
Employment income				
Property income				
Building society interest				
Dividend income				
Net income				
Less personal allowance				
Taxable income				

4 Restricting the personal allowance

4.1 The basic calculation

If an individual has net income in excess of £100,000 then the personal allowance must be reduced.

It is reduced by £1 for every £2 income the taxpayer has over the £100,000 limit.

The personal allowance may be reduced to £0 if income is greater than or equal to £125,000.

Formula to learn

Restriction = ½ (Net income – 100,000) [limit but no formula given in CBT].

Illustration 4: Personal allowance restriction

In 2020/21, Kelvin has gross employment income of £98,000 and receives building society interest of £1,500 and dividends of £5,000. Kelvin's net income for 2020/21 is:

	Non-savings income £	Savings income £	Dividend income £	Total £
Net income	98,000	1,500	5,000	104,500

The total is above the adjustment threshold of £100,000 so we must reduce the personal allowance.

	£
Net income	104,500
Less income limit	(100,000)
Excess	4,500
Personal allowance	12,500
Less half excess (4,500/2)	(2,250)
Adjusted personal allowance	10,250

The taxable income is therefore:

	Non-savings income £	Savings income £	Dividend income £	Total £
Net income	98,000	1,500	5,000	104,500
Less personal allowance	(10,250)	–	–	(10,250)
Taxable income	87,750	1,500	5,000	94,250

Activity 3: Personal allowance restriction

Karen has net income of £107,000 (all non-savings income).

Required

What personal allowance does Karen receive for 2020/21, and what is her taxable income?

Solution

Her personal allowance is | £ |

Her taxable income is | £ |

4.2 Charitable donations/pension payments

If a taxpayer makes Gift Aid or personal pension scheme contributions in the year (see next chapter), then they are allowed to deduct the payments from net income before calculating the restriction on the personal allowance.

Both of these payments are made net by the taxpayer but it is the gross amount that is deducted from the net income. We will consider this in detail in the next chapter.

Total income after deducting Gift Aid and personal pension contributions is called **adjusted net income**.

Note. Gift Aid and personal pension contributions are only deducted from total income for the purpose of calculating the personal allowance; they are not deducted from income in the tax computation.

Illustration 5: Personal allowance restriction with Gift Aid payment

As per Illustration 4 in 2020/21, Kelvin has gross employment income of £98,000 and receives building society interest of £1,500 and dividends of £5,000. However, he now makes a gross payment to charity of £1,000 under Gift Aid. Kelvin's net income for 2020/21 is still:

	Non-savings income £	Savings income £	Dividend income £	Total £
Net income	98,000	1,500	5,000	104,500

The total is above the adjustment threshold of £100,000 so we must reduce the personal allowance. However, as he has made a payment to charity under Gift Aid we are allowed to reduce the net income before calculating the restriction:

	£
Net income	104,500
Less gross Gift Aid payment	(1,000)
Adjusted net income	103,500
Less income limit	(100,000)
Excess	3,500
Personal allowance	12,500
Less half excess (3,500/2)	(1,750)
Adjusted personal allowance	10,750

The taxable income is therefore:

	Non-savings income £	Savings income £	Dividend income £	Total £
Net income	98,000	1,500	5,000	104,500
Less personal allowance	(10,750)	–	–	(10,750)
Taxable income	87,250	1,500	5,000	93,750

Activity 4: Personal allowance with personal pension payment

Karen, who has net income of £107,000, now makes a personal pension payment of £2,000 gross.

Required

What personal allowance will Karen receive? What is her taxable income?

Solution

Her personal allowance is £ [   ]

Her taxable income is £ [   ]

We will revisit Gift Aid and personal pension payments in the next chapter.

5 Tax planning

Individuals will pay different rates of tax depending on the level of their income. If possible, married couples and civil partners should consider whether cash balances yielding interest and shares yielding dividends could be held by taxpayers paying the lower rate of tax or having unused personal allowances (see Chapter 2).

Other matters to consider:

- Taxpayers could invest in products that yield exempt income such as ISAs or premium bonds.

- Taxpayers could make payments into personal pension schemes or payments to charity under Gift Aid to preserve their entitlement to the personal allowance (see Chapter 2).

Chapter summary

- There are three types of income in the income tax computation: non-savings, savings and dividend.

- Non-savings income includes employment income, property income, trading (or business) income and pension income.

- Savings income is interest received.

- Dividend income is dividends received.

- Exempt income includes income from individual savings accounts (ISAs) and gambling winnings.

- Tax computations must be prepared for a tax year.

- All the components of an individual's income are added together to arrive at 'net income'.

- Net income less the personal allowance gives 'taxable income'.

- The personal allowance is deducted first from non-savings income, then from savings income and finally from dividend income. It is reduced by £1 for every £2 that the individual's net income exceeds the income limit of £100,000.

- The net income figure for comparison to the income limit for the personal allowance is reduced by gross Gift Aid donations and personal pension contributions.

Keywords

- **Dividend income:** Dividends received from a company
- **Net income:** An individual's total income calculated prior to deducting the personal allowance
- **Non-savings income:** Income other than interest and dividends
- **Personal allowance:** The amount of income a taxpayer may receive before paying tax
- **Savings income:** Interest received, for example from a bank or building society
- **Taxable income:** An individual's net income minus the personal allowance
- **Total income:** Technically a different sub-total to net income but in your syllabus the terms may be used interchangeably

1 **Classify the following types of income by ticking the correct box:**

	Non-savings income	Savings income	Dividend income
Employment income			
Dividends			
Property income			
Bank interest			
Pension income			
Interest on government stock			

2 **Complete the table below to show the amount of income that would be included in a tax return for 2020/21. If your answer is zero, please put a '0'.**

	Amount received £	Amount in tax return £
Building society interest	240	
Interest on an individual savings account	40	
Dividends	160	
Interest from government gilts	350	

3 In 2020/21, Joe has employment income of £30,000 and receives dividends of £300 and premium bond winnings of £500.

Use the table below to show his taxable income for 2020/21.

	Non-savings income £	Dividend income £	Total £

4 Pratish receives property income of £3,000 and building society interest of £9,000 in 2020/21.

Use the table below to show his taxable income for 2020/21.

	Non-savings income £	Savings income £	Total £

5 Jesse has employment income of £112,200 in 2020/21. He also received building society interest of £5,000, a prize of £50 in an internet competition and dividends of £4,000.

Use the table below to show Jesse's taxable income for 2020/21.

	Non-savings income £	Savings income £	Dividend income £	Total £

Calculation of income tax

2

Learning outcomes

2	Calculate a UK taxpayer's total income
2.2	Calculate income from investments • Personal savings allowance • Dividend allowance
3	Calculate income tax and National Insurance (NI) contributions payable by a UK taxpayer
3.2	Apply relief for pension payments and charitable donations • Apply occupational pension schemes • Apply private pension schemes • Apply charitable donations
3.3	Perform income tax computations • Calculate income tax, combining all income into one schedule • Apply tax rates and bands • Deduct income tax at source
3.5	Advise on tax planning techniques to minimise tax liabilities • Maximise relevant exemptions and reliefs • Change investment incomes to make them more tax efficient • Make other changes that can minimise tax liabilities

Assessment context

Task 6 of the initial AAT sample assessment required you to perform a detailed income tax calculation as well do a separate question on personal allowance restriction. 12 marks were available.

Qualification context

If you are studying *Business Tax*, then the material in this chapter will be useful background but you will not be tested on these areas outside of this unit.

Business context

Calculating income tax payable is the main task a tax adviser will perform for their client.

Chapter overview

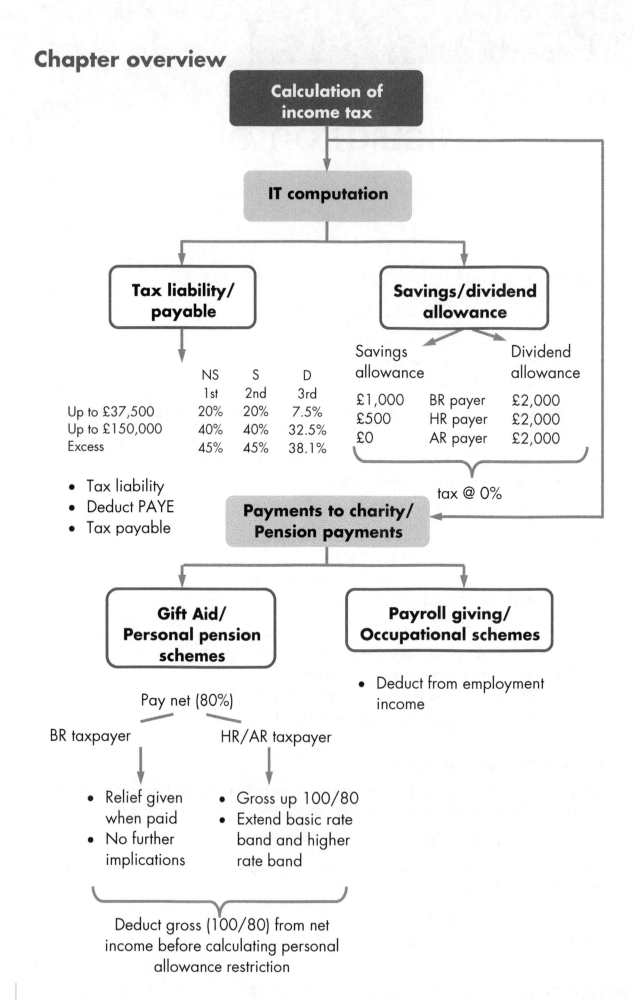

Introduction

The calculation of income tax will appear complex at first. There is a set of basic rules but these can be applied in many different combinations depending on a taxpayer's circumstances, meaning there are many different scenarios for you to get to grips with.

In this chapter we will consider some, but not all, of the possible scenarios. The more examples you study and questions you attempt the more familiar you will become with how the rules operate.

1 Calculation of income tax liability

Income tax is calculated at different rates depending on the type and level of income the taxpayer has.

The various rates for 2020/21 are summarised in the diagram below. This data will be provided for you in the taxation tables in your assessment.

The taxable income we calculated in the previous chapter is taxed in the following order:

(a) Non-savings income
(b) Savings income
(c) Dividend income

So, on the diagram we move from left to right.

Illustration 1: Calculation of tax liability

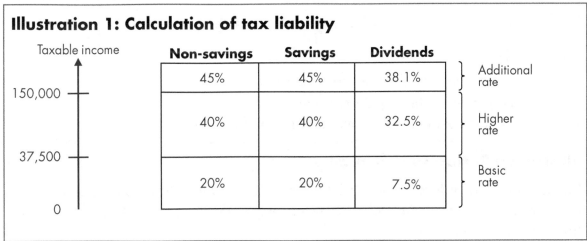

Note. we have different **tax bands**.

The basic rate band covers income from £1 to £37,500.

The **higher rate band** covers income from £37,501 to £150,000.

The **additional rate band** covers income over £150,000.

These bands may be adjusted for taxpayers who make payments to charity under Gift Aid or pay into a personal pension scheme.

In addition to these bands, there is a **personal savings allowance** that applies to savings income and a **dividend allowance** that applies to dividend income.

We apply these rates to give us our **income tax liability**.

Income tax liability is total amount of tax that should be paid on our income.

Don't forget that an employed taxpayer will have had income tax deducted from their salary before it has been paid to them. This represents an estimated prepayment of income tax for the year. We deduct this from the income tax liability to see whether there is any further **income tax payable** for the year.

It is possible that the taxpayer has paid too much tax. If they have there will be **income tax repayable**.

Income tax payable Outstanding income tax due for the tax year.

Income tax repayable Income tax due to the taxpayer because they have overpaid.

Assessment focus point

Read the requirement very carefully to see if you are being asked to calculate **income tax liability** or **income tax payable**. You will lose marks or waste time if you calculate the wrong one.

2 Taxation of non-savings income

Non-savings income is taxed first.

- It is taxed initially in the basic rate band at 20%.
- It is then taxed in the higher rate band at 40%.
- Finally, it is taxed in the additional rate band at 45%.

Illustration 2: Non-saving income

Nathan has taxable income of £185,000 (>£125,000 therefore no personal allowance) consisting entirely of non-savings employment income. PAYE of £65,000 has been deducted.

The non-savings income uses all the basic rate band of £37,500, the next £112,500 of income falls into the higher rate band and the excess above that falls into the additional rate band.

The income tax liability is:

	Income tax £
Non-savings income	
37,500 × 20%	7,500
112,500 × 40%	45,000
35,000 × 45%	15,750
185,000	
Income tax liability	68,250
Less PAYE	(65,000)
Income tax payable	3,250

This can be illustrated on the diagram as follows:

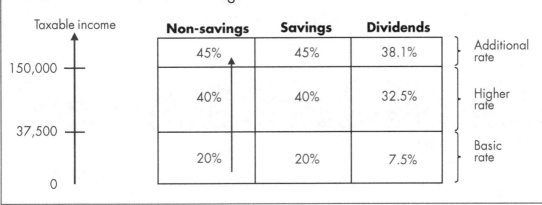

3 Savings income

Once we have taxed non-savings income we then move on to tax savings income.

We begin taxing savings income in the bands at the point where we finished taxing the non-savings income. So in the previous illustration (Illustration 2) Nathan would pay tax on any savings income in the additional rate band as he has already used his basic rate and higher rate band.

Savings income is taxed as follows:

- At 20% on any savings falling in the basic rate band
- At 40% on any savings falling in the higher rate band
- At 45% on any savings falling in the additional rate band

However, there is a further complication in that taxpayers will potentially receive the **personal savings allowance**. This represents savings income that is taxed at 0%. Taxpayers receive the personal savings allowance as follows:

A basic rate taxpayer (one who has adjusted net income of less than £50,000) receives a personal savings allowance of £1,000.

A higher rate taxpayer (one who has adjusted net income greater than £50,000 but no more than £150,000) receives a personal savings allowance of £500.

An additional rate taxpayer (one who has adjusted net income greater than £150,000) does not receive a personal savings allowance.

(You will note these thresholds represent the relevant bands plus the personal allowance where this is available so for example the basic rate test is £37,500 plus £12,500 equals £50,000, the higher rate test is £150,000 plus £0 as no personal allowance would be available for a taxpayer with £150,000 worth of income.)

Illustration 3: Savings income example 1

Sasha has net income of £42,620 (before the personal allowance) and taxable income of £30,120. Of this, £18,920 is non-savings income and £11,200 is savings income.

Her net income is less than £50,000 so she is a basic rate taxpayer. She is therefore entitled to a personal savings allowance of £1,000.

Her non-savings income will use up some of the basic rate band. As a basic rate taxpayer, she will pay income tax on her savings income in excess of the personal savings allowance at 20%.

The income tax liability is:

	Income tax £
Non-savings income	
18,920 × 20%	3,784
Savings income	
1,000 × 0% (personal savings allowance)	0
10,200 × 20% (11,200 − 1,000)	2,040
Income tax liability	5,824

This can be illustrated on the diagram as below.

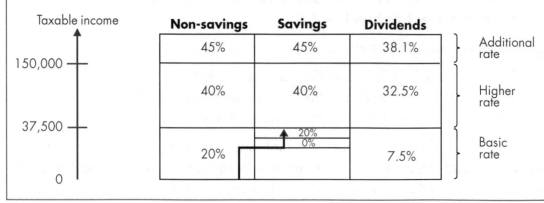

Illustration 4: Savings income example 2

Dave has net income of £91,500 (before the personal allowance) and taxable income of £79,000. Of this, £70,000 is non-savings income and £9,000 is savings income.

His net income is greater than £50,000 but less than £150,000 so he is a higher rate taxpayer. He is therefore entitled to a personal savings allowance of £500.

His non-savings income will use up all of the basic rate band. He will therefore pay income tax on his savings income in excess of the personal savings allowance at 40%.

The income tax liability is:

	Income tax £
Non-savings income	
37,500 × 20%	7,500
32,500 × 40% (70,000 − 37,500)	13,000
Savings income	
500 × 0% (personal savings allowance)	0
8,500 × 40% (9,000 − 500)	3,400
Income tax liability	23,900

This can be illustrated on the diagram below.

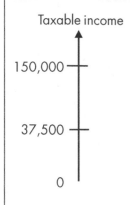

Taxable income	Non-savings	Savings	Dividends	
150,000	45%	45%	38.1%	Additional rate
	40%	40% / 0%	32.5%	Higher rate
37,500	20%	20%	7.5%	Basic rate
0				

Illustration 5: Savings income example 3

Frank has net income of £180,000. He receives no personal allowance so his taxable income is also £180,000. Of this, £100,000 is non-savings income and £80,000 is savings income.

His net income is greater than £150,000 so he is an additional rate taxpayer. He is therefore not entitled to a personal savings allowance.

His non-savings income will use up all of the basic rate band. He will therefore pay income tax on his savings income initially at 40% and then 45%.

The income tax liability is:

	Income tax £
Non-savings income	
37,500 × 20%	7,500
62,500 × 40% (100,000 – 37,500)	25,000
Savings income	
50,000 × 40% (150,000 – 37,500 – 62,500)	20,000
30,000 × 45% (80,000 – 50,000)	13,500
£180,000	
Income tax liability	66,000

This can be illustrated on the diagram below.

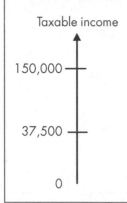

Activity 1: Income tax liability

In 2020/21 Jules, who is single, has employment income of £39,000 and building society interest of £9,000.

Required

Calculate the income tax liability.

Solution

	Non-savings income £	Savings income £	Total £

4 Dividend income

Once we have taxed non-savings income and savings income, we then move on to tax dividend income.

As before, we begin taxing dividend income in the bands at the point where we finished taxing the savings income.

Dividend income is taxed as follows:

- At 7.5% on any dividend income falling in the basic rate band
- At 32.5% on any dividend income falling in the higher rate band
- At 38.1% on any dividend income falling in the additional rate band

However, there is a further complication in that taxpayers will receive the dividend allowance. This represents dividend income that is taxed at 0%. All taxpayers receive a dividend allowance of £2,000 regardless of their level of net income.

Illustration 6: Dividend income

Douglas has net income of £165,000. Of this, £120,000 is non-savings income, £20,000 is savings income and £25,000 is dividend income.

Douglas is clearly an additional rate taxpayer so he will not receive a personal savings allowance. However, he is entitled to the dividend allowance.

The non-savings income of £120,000 uses all the basic rate band and some of the higher rate band. The £20,000 interest uses a further £20,000 of the higher rate band, leaving a balance of £10,000 remaining. The first £2,000 of dividend income is taxed at 0% because of the dividend allowance but this uses up £2,000 of the remaining higher rate band, leaving £8,000 available for the dividend. The next £8,000 of dividend is therefore taxed in the higher rate band at 32.5%, with the balance of £15,000 taxed at 38.1%.

The income tax liability is:

	Income tax £
Non-savings income	
37,500 × 20%	7,500
82,500 × 40%	33,000
Savings income	
20,000 × 40%	8,000
Dividend income	
2,000 × 0% (dividend allowance)	0
8,000 × 32.5%	2,600
15,000 × 38.1% (25,000 – 2,000 – 8,000)	5,715
Income tax liability	56,815

This can be illustrated on the diagram below.

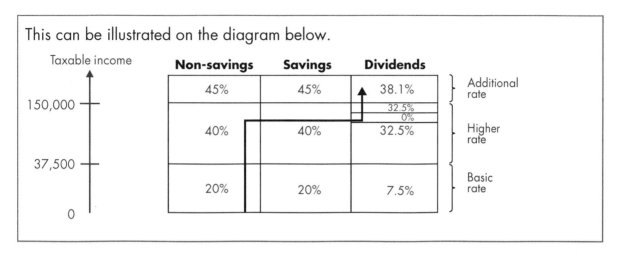

Activity 2: Income tax payable

Arthur has a salary of £125,000 (PAYE £42,000). He received bank interest of £10,000 and dividends of £10,000.

Required

Calculate the net income tax payable for 2020/21.

Solution

	Non-savings income £	Savings income £	Dividend income £	Total £

	Non-savings income £	Savings income £	Dividend income £	Total £

5 Extending the bands

Certain donations to UK registered charities or payments into personal pension schemes are eligible for tax relief.

Essentially, the income the taxpayer puts into the pension scheme/gives to charity is not taxable. The taxpayer therefore saves the tax they would have paid on that income.

Different taxpayers will therefore be entitled to relief at different rates.

Most taxpayers are employees who have already paid their tax via PAYE. By giving money to charity/paying into a pension they are therefore entitled to a refund of tax already paid on this income. Most taxpayers pay tax at 20% so making a payment of £100 would entitle them to a repayment of £20.

It would be onerous for the taxpayer and the Government if everyone who made such a payment had to apply to the Government for a tax refund so to simplify the administration payments are always made **net** of basic rate (20%) tax. The charity/pension will then reclaim the 20% tax from HMRC on behalf of all its donors in one go, saving much time and effort.

The taxpayer has therefore obtained relief at 20% as the charity/pension receives the full 100% but it has only cost the taxpayer 80%. This is effectively the same as the taxpayer giving the charity/pension 100% and then claiming the 20% tax back from the Government that they have already paid on that income.

If the taxpayer does pay tax at 20% then no further action is required on their part.

Higher rate (40%) taxpayers are entitled to an additional 20% (40% – 20%) relief on their gross donation/pension contribution. Additional rate taxpayers are entitled to an additional 25% (45% – 20%) relief on their gross donation/pension contribution.

Additional (20% or 25%) relief is given for charitable donations/pension contributions made by higher/additional rate taxpayers by a process known as 'extending the bands'. This moves income that would have been taxed at a higher rate into a lower rate band, effectively giving the taxpayer a discount on their tax bill.

The basic rate upper limit becomes:

> 37,500 + (payments × 100/80) – income is moved out of higher rate into basic rate saving 20% (40% – 20%)

The higher rate limit becomes:

> 150,000 + (payment × 100/80) – income is moved out of additional rate into higher rate saving a further 5% (45% – 40%). This combined with the basic rate extension above gives the taxpayer a 25% saving (20% + 5%).

Assessment focus point

If a taxpayer makes a payment to charity under Gift Aid or makes a payment into a personal pension scheme, gross up the amount paid by 100/80 and then add this total to the basic rate and higher rate band before calculating the tax liability.

Double check that the figure has not been given to you gross in the question. If it is already gross don't gross it up again.

Illustration 7: Gift Aid donation

Gustav has taxable income (all non-savings) of £50,000 in 2020/21.

Assuming that Gustav does not make any Gift Aid donations or personal pension contributions in 2020/21 his income tax liability will be:

	£
37,500 × 20%	7,500
12,500 × 40%	5,000
50,000	12,500

Now think about the situation where Gustav makes a Gift Aid donation of £8,000 in 2020/21. The Gift Aid donation will have been paid net of 20% tax. This means that the gross amount of the payment is £8,000 × 100/80 = £10,000 and Gustav's basic rate band must be extended by £10,000. His income tax liability is calculated as follows:

	£
37,500 × 20%	7,500
10,000 (extended basic rate band) × 20%	2,000
2,500 × 40%	1,000
50,000	10,500

Extending the basic rate band means that £10,000 more income is taxed at the basic rate and therefore £10,000 less income is taxed at the higher rate. The difference between the tax liabilities with and without the Gift Aid donation is £10,000 × (40 − 20)% = £2,000. The total tax relief is:

	£
Basic rate relief given by net payment (10,000 − 8,000)	2,000
Higher rate relief given by extending basic rate band	2,000
Total tax relief (which equates to 40% of the gross donation)	4,000

Activity 3: Tax liability with Gift Aid donation

In 2020/21, Charlie has employment income of £100,000. He wishes to make a donation of £8,000 (net) to charity.

Required

For 2020/21, calculate Charlie's:

(a) **Taxable income**

£ _____

(b) **Tax liability if he does not make the donation**

£ _____

(c) Tax liability if he does make the donation

£

(d) Total tax saved if he does make the donation

£

Remember that a personal pension contribution or Gift Aid payment is deducted from total income before restricting the personal allowance. It is the **gross** payment that is deducted (payment $\times$ 100/80).

6 Payroll giving and occupational pension schemes

A taxpayer may also donate to charity via their employer. Under payroll giving, the taxpayer requests that their employer pay some of their salary directly to charity.

A taxpayer may contribute to an occupational pension scheme. This is a pension scheme provided by the employer. Contributions will be deducted directly from the employee's salary.

The taxpayer will obtain tax relief on both of these payments. As they are deducted from salary, they reduce the taxpayer's taxable income and thus their tax liability.

Taxpayers will save at either 20%, 40% or 45% depending on their level of income.

There is no need to extend the basic rate band for these payments.

7 Tax planning

Even if both people in a marriage/civil partnership pay tax at the same rate they should consider transferring assets between each other to ensure they get the maximum benefit from the savings allowance and the dividend allowance. For example if each person is paying tax at higher rate they will each receive a personal savings allowance of £500. If one party owns all the invested cash and is in receipt of £1,000 of interest then £500 of it will be above the allowance and will be taxable. If half of the cash is transferred to the other party then they will both be in receipt of £500 which will be covered by their personal savings allowance and together they will not pay tax.

People should also consider making charitable payments or payments into pensions to reduce their tax liability or to preserve the higher personal savings allowance. Again, with couples it makes more sense for the taxpayer paying tax at the higher rate to make the payment.

Chapter summary

- Income is categorised into different types: non-savings, savings and dividend. Each type of income suffers different rates of tax, depending on whether the income falls into the basic or higher rate bands or over the additional rate threshold.

- Non-savings income is taxed first (at 20%, then 40%, then 45%) then savings income (at 20%, then 40%, then 45%) and finally dividend income (at 7.5%, then 32.5%, then 38.1%).

- A personal savings allowance is available at £1,000 for a basic rate taxpayer, £500 for a higher rate taxpayer and £0 for an additional rate taxpayer. Savings income falling into the allowance is taxed at 0%. The allowance uses up the basic rate and higher rate band.

- A dividend allowance of £2,000 is available to all taxpayers. Dividends falling into this band are taxed at 0%. The allowance uses up the basic rate and higher rate bands.

- Gift Aid donations and personal pension contributions are paid net of basic rate (20%) tax.

- Extend the basic rate band by the gross amount of any Gift Aid donations and/or personal pension contributions paid by the taxpayer. This gives further tax relief to higher and additional rate taxpayers.

- Payments made to charity via payroll deduction or pension contributions made to an occupational scheme are simply deducted from salary.

- Tax deducted under the PAYE system is deducted in computing tax payable and can be repaid if it is greater than the taxpayer's liability.

Keywords

- **Additional rate band:** Income in excess of £150,000 is taxed here

- **Basic rate band:** The first £37,500 of taxable income. The basic rate band may be extended by the gross amount of any Gift Aid donations and personal pension contributions paid by the taxpayer

- **Dividend allowance:** An amount of savings income that is taxed at 0%. This is £2,000 for all taxpayers

- **Higher rate band:** The next £112,500 of taxable income. The upper limit to the higher rate band may be extended by the gross amount of any Gift Aid donations and personal pension contributions paid

- **Personal savings allowance:** An amount of savings income that is taxed at 0%. The amount varies depending on levels of income

1   At what rates is income tax charged on non-savings income?

Tick ONE box.

	✓
0%, 20%, 40% and 45%	
40% and 45%	
20% only	
20%, 40% and 45%	

2   In 2020/21 Albert has a salary of £17,450, £2,000 of building society interest and £3,000 of dividends.

Albert's income tax liability is:

£ [   ]

3   In 2020/21 Harry has a salary of £140,000, and has received building society interest of £20,000 and dividends of £30,000.

Harry's income tax liability is:

£ [   ]

4   **Explain how tax relief is given on Gift Aid donations.**

5   Doreen has the following sources of income in 2020/21.

	£
Gross pension income (tax deducted under PAYE £1,850)	17,000
Property income	4,350
Interest received from government stock	380
Dividends received	700
Premium bond prize	100

Calculate Doreen's income tax payable or repayable for the year.

6   Sase has the following income and outgoings in 2020/21.

	£
Business profits	39,600
Building society interest received	2,000
Dividends received	12,000
Gift Aid donation paid	1,600

Compute Sase's income tax payable for the year.

7   Vince is a higher rate taxpayer and makes a Gift Aid donation of £15,000 in 2020/21.

What is Vince's basic rate band in 2020/21?

Tick ONE box.

	✓
£37,500	
£52,500	
£56,250	
£62,500	

Employment income

3

Learning outcomes

2	Calculate a UK taxpayer's total income
2.1	**Calculate income from employment** • Calculate employment income, including salaries, pension income, wages, commissions and bonuses • Calculate taxable benefits in kind • Identify exempt benefits in kind • Identify and calculate allowable and exempt expenses
3	**Calculate income tax and National Insurance (NI) contributions payable by a UK taxpayer**
3.2	**Apply relief for pension payments and charitable donations** • Apply occupational pension schemes • Apply private pension schemes
3.5	**Advise on tax planning techniques to minimise tax liabilities** • Change benefits in kind to make them more tax efficient

Assessment context

Benefits are highly examinable. Make sure you can calculate and explain them. In the initial AAT sample assessment Task 2 tested the rules on car benefits for 8 marks. Task 3 tested other benefits for 8 marks. Task 6 required you to perform a detailed income tax calculation for 12 marks and so in your assessment a brief employment income working could form part of this task. Task 8 tested a number of sundry matters for 7 marks, one of the questions related to quantifying the difference in tax an employee would pay if they chose one benefit over another.

Qualification context

You will not see the information in this chapter outside of this unit.

Business context

You will not see these areas again in your AAT qualification outside of this unit.

Chapter overview

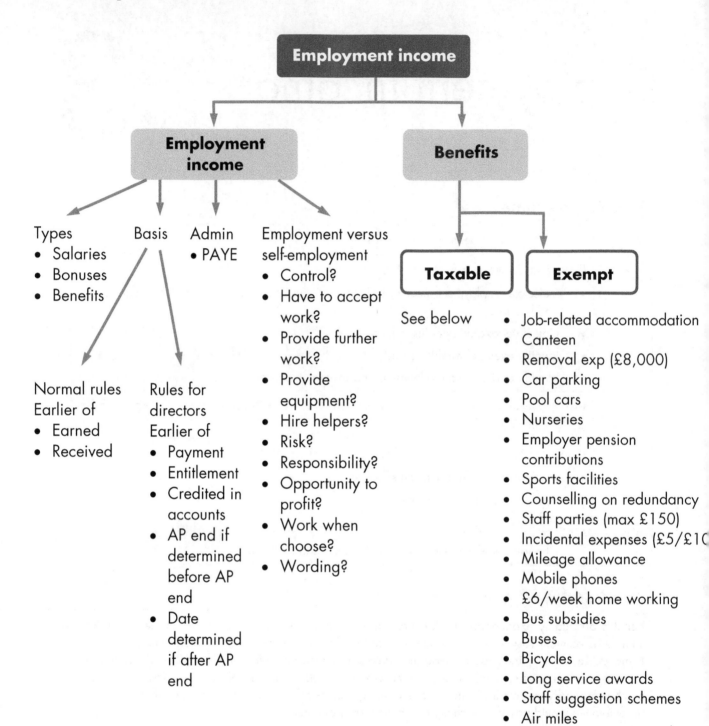

Employment income

Employment income

Types
- Salaries
- Bonuses
- Benefits

Basis

Admin
- PAYE

Employment versus self-employment
- Control?
- Have to accept work?
- Provide further work?
- Provide equipment?
- Hire helpers?
- Risk?
- Responsibility?
- Opportunity to profit?
- Work when choose?
- Wording?

Normal rules
Earlier of
- Earned
- Received

Rules for directors
Earlier of
- Payment
- Entitlement
- Credited in accounts
- AP end if determined before AP end
- Date determined if after AP end

Benefits

Taxable

See below

Exempt

- Job-related accommodation
- Canteen
- Removal exp (£8,000)
- Car parking
- Pool cars
- Nurseries
- Employer pension contributions
- Sports facilities
- Counselling on redundancy
- Staff parties (max £150)
- Incidental expenses (£5/£10)
- Mileage allowance
- Mobile phones
- £6/week home working
- Bus subsidies
- Buses
- Bicycles
- Long service awards
- Staff suggestion schemes
- Air miles
- Training
- Taxis
- £250 third-party gifts
- Gifts outside of employment
- Payment or reimbursement of allowable business expenses

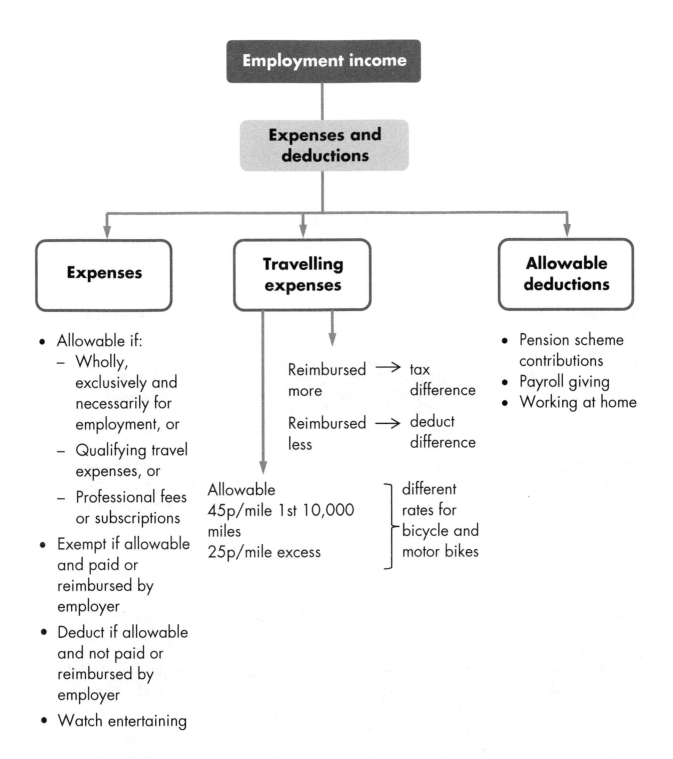

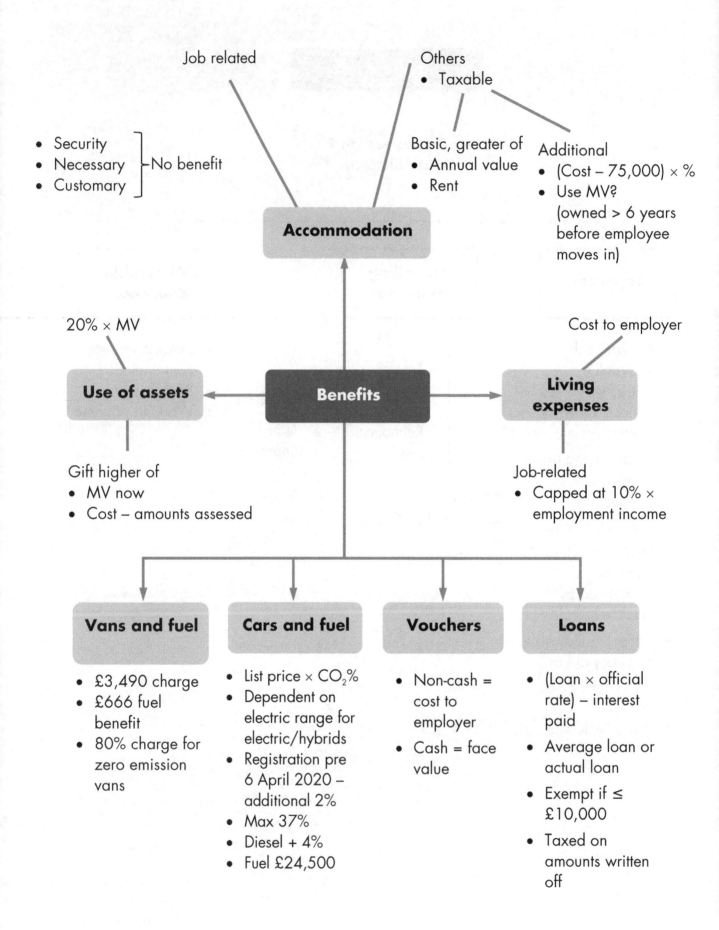

Job related

Others
- Taxable

Security
Necessary — No benefit
Customary

Basic, greater of
- Annual value
- Rent

Additional
- (Cost – 75,000) × %
- Use MV?
(owned > 6 years
before employee
moves in)

Accommodation

20% × MV

Use of assets ← **Benefits** → **Living expenses**

Cost to employer

Gift higher of
- MV now
- Cost – amounts assessed

Job-related
- Capped at 10% ×
employment income

Vans and fuel

- £3,490 charge
- £666 fuel benefit
- 80% charge for zero emission vans

Cars and fuel

- List price × CO_2%
- Dependent on electric range for electric/hybrids
- Registration pre 6 April 2020 – additional 2%
- Max 37%
- Diesel + 4%
- Fuel £24,500

Vouchers

- Non-cash = cost to employer
- Cash = face value

Loans

- (Loan × official rate) – interest paid
- Average loan or actual loan
- Exempt if ≤ £10,000
- Taxed on amounts written off

Introduction

Before we can calculate the income tax that an individual will pay we have to calculate their total income.

Their total income will be made up of income from different sources; for example a person renting out property will have **property income**, while a person who is employed will have **employment income**.

Different types of income are calculated in different ways.

In this chapter we are going to look at how to calculate employment income.

Note that a great deal of the information in this chapter is provided in the assessment in the tax tables.

1 Employment income

Key term

> **Employment income** This is the type of income received by someone who holds an office or employment. It is calculated using the detailed rules we will be considering in this chapter.

It is usually clear whether someone is employed or self-employed. If you work for the same person every working day for a regular salary then you are employed. If you pay, say, a plumber to perform some work for you then they are self-employed; they are not your employee.

However, in certain circumstances it is not obvious whether a taxpayer is an employee or self-employed. It is important to classify the relationship correctly otherwise the wrong tax rules would be applied.

HMRC would consider whether the taxpayer has a **contract of service** or **a contract for services**.

A contract of service means the taxpayer works for the other party over a period of time, performing different tasks as they are assigned to them. The relationship is ongoing. This makes them employed.

A contract for services means the taxpayer has agreed to perform a specific task or tasks. Once these tasks have been completed the relationship is at an end. This makes them self-employed.

If it is not clear whether we have a contract of service or contract for services then HMRC would consider the following:

(a) The degree of control exercised over the person doing the work – control implies an employment relationship

(b) Whether they must accept further work – obligation implies employment

(c) Whether the other party must provide further work – obligation implies employment

(d) Whether they provide their own equipment – using someone else's equipment implies an employment relationship

(e) Whether they hire their own helpers – hiring their own helpers suggests autonomy meaning they are self-employed

(f) What degree of financial risk they take – self-employment is more risky than employment

(g) What degree of responsibility for investment and management they have – self-employed people have more responsibility than employed people

(h) Whether they can profit from sound management – self-employed people will benefit directly from good decisions they make

(i) Whether they can work when they choose – self-employed people have more flexibility over how they work

(j) The wording used in any agreement between the parties – this will help us to understand the nature of the relationship

In this unit we are only concerned with the taxation of employed people. The calculation of income from self-employment is a major part of the *Business Tax* syllabus.

2 Taxation of employment income

2.1 Types of income

A taxpayer will be taxed on any amounts deriving from an office or employment performed wholly or partly in the UK including:

- Salaries, bonuses and commissions
- Non-cash benefits, for example a company car
- Payments made on termination of employment

2.2 Basis of assessment

These rules identify the tax year that income is taxed in. There are normal rules and additional rules that apply to directors only.

2.2.1 Normal rules

A taxpayer will be assessed on amounts received in the current tax year (6 April 2020–5 April 2021).

Earnings are treated as received at the earlier of:

- The time when payment is made
- The time when a person becomes entitled to payment of the earnings

Illustration 1: Basis of assessment

Joy is employed by R plc. She is entitled to the payment of a bonus of £2,000 on 31 March 2021, although she does not receive it until 25 April 2021.

Joy will be taxed on the bonus in 2020/21 because she is entitled to payment on 31 March 2021.

If the bonus payment to Joy was calculated based on the results of R plc for 31 March 2021 but she was not entitled to it at that date, she would be taxed on receipt of the bonus in 2021/22 or on the date she actually becomes entitled to it, if earlier.

Activity 1: Basis of assessment

Rudolph is an employee of Mabuse Ltd. He earns a salary of £28,000 (paid monthly on the last working day of each month) but on 1 November 2020 he is promoted and his salary increases to £35,000. The company also pays him a bonus relating to the year ended 31 March 2020 of £3,000 on 15 May 2020. The bonus for the year ended 31 March 2021 of £4,000 is paid on 13 May 2021.

Required

(a) What is Rudolph's taxable salary for 2020/21?

£ [ ]

(b) What is Rudolph's taxable bonus for 2020/21?

£ [ ]

2.2.2 Rules for directors

Special rules apply to company directors. Their earnings are treated as being received on the earliest of:

- The time when payment is made
- The time when a person becomes entitled to payment of the earnings
- The time when the amount is credited in the company's accounting records
- The end of the company's period of account (if the amount has been determined by then)
- The time the amount is determined (if after the end of the company's period of account)

2.3 Deduction of tax by employers

Employers have an obligation to deduct income tax from payments they make to their employees under the **Pay As You Earn (PAYE) system**. Tax is deducted on both cash payments and benefits. Employees therefore receive their salary net of tax.

Most employees will have the correct amount of tax deducted by their employers so there will be no need for them to complete a tax return or make further payments of tax.

In your assessment salaries will be quoted gross. This means you are given the figure before tax has been deducted. You will then be provided with information as to the amount of income tax deducted under PAYE.

3 Taxable benefits

Certain perks provided by employers represent **benefits** taxable on employees. The rules on these are set out in legislation called the **benefits code**.

There are specific rules applying to certain benefits, for example cars. If there is no specific rule then employees will be taxed on the cost to the employer of providing the benefit.

As a general rule:

- There is no taxable benefit if there is no private benefit to the employee (eg no benefit for the use of a projector in class by a BPP tutor)

- Time apportion the benefit if it is not available for the whole tax year

- Deduct any contributions made by the employee from the benefit

3.1 Cars

A car provided by the employer that is available for private use gives rise to a benefit. If fuel is provided for private motoring there will be an additional benefit.

Note that HMRC considers commuting to work and back as private use so in practice if an employee uses a car belonging to their employer they will normally be taxed on this as a benefit. The exception to this would be a **pool car** (see later).

3.1.1 Car benefit

The starting point for calculating a car benefit is the list price of the car. A percentage of that list price is the taxable benefit.

The price of the car is calculated as follows:

- List price when new*, plus optional extras costing at least £100
- Deduct capital contributions made by employee (capped at £5,000)

* Ignore any discounts that have been obtained; it is the published list price which is relevant.

The percentage used varies, depending on the CO_2 emissions, the electric range for hybrid cars and whether the car is petrol- or diesel-fuelled. In addition, cars registered before 6 April 2020 will be subject to a 2% higher rate.

 Assessment focus point

CO_2 g/km	Electric range (miles)	Electric/ hybrid	Petrol engine (a)	Diesel engine (a) (b)
Nil		0%		
>0 ≤ 50 g/km	130 or more	0%		
>0 ≤ 50 g/km	70-129	3%		
>0 ≤ 50 g/km	40-69	6%		
>0 ≤ 50 g/km	30-39	10%		
>0 ≤ 50 g/km	Less than 30	12%		
>50 ≤ 54 g/km			13%	17%
≥ 55 g/km			Calculation: Minimum 14% Maximum 37%	Calculation: Minimum 18% Maximum 37%

(a) For cars registered prior to 6 April 2020, add 2% to the above rates. The question would specify the registration date if relevant.

(b) Diesel engine cars registered after 1 September 2017 and meeting the RDE2 standards will use the same rates as petrol engine cars. The question would specify if this was met.

 Formula provided

For cars that emit CO_2 of more than 54 g/km, the taxable benefit percentage starts at 14% and increases by 1% for every 5 g/km (rounded down to the nearest multiple of 5) by which CO_2 emissions exceed 55 g/km, up to a maximum of 37%.

BPP
LEARNING MEDIA

Illustration 2: Car benefit percentage

Working for a car with CO_2 emissions > 54 g/km

The relevant CO_2 percentage for a petrol car registered on or after 6 April 2020 with 168 g/km CO_2 emissions is calculated as follows:

Round down to 165

165 – 55 = 110

Divided by 5 = 22

Add basic 14 + 22 = 36%

Diesel cars have a supplement of 4%. The maximum benefit, however, remains 37% of the list price. The supplement does not apply if the car is registered after 1 September 2017 and meets the RDE2 emissions standards (as mentioned above).

The benefit is apportioned if the car is not available for the whole year or cannot be used for a period of at least 30 days (for example if being repaired).

The benefit is reduced by any payment the user must make for the private use of the car (as distinct from a one-off capital contribution to the cost of the car which would be deducted from the price before applying the percentage).

Pool cars are exempt. A car is a pool car if all the following conditions are satisfied:

- It is used by more than one employee/director and not ordinarily used by one of them to the exclusion of others.

- Any private use is incidental to business use.

- Not normally kept overnight at or near the residence of an employee.

3.1.2 Fuel benefit

Where fuel is provided for private miles (including commuting) there is a further benefit in addition to the car benefit.

The taxable benefit is a percentage of a base figure. The base figure for 2020/21 is £24,500 (see tax tables).

The percentage is the same percentage as is used to calculate the car benefit.

Assessment focus point

Exceptionally there is no reduction in benefit for contributions made by the employee – don't get caught out by this!

There is no benefit if the employee pays for all private fuel.

Illustration 3: Car and fuel benefit

An employee was provided with a new petrol engine car costing £15,000 (the list price) on 6 June 2020. The car was first registered in May 2020. During 2020/21, the employer spent £900 on insurance, repairs and the vehicle licence. The firm paid for all petrol (£2,300) without reimbursement. The employee was required to pay the firm £25 per month for the private use of the car. The car has CO_2 emissions of 82 g/km.

The total taxable benefit for 2020/21 in respect of the car and fuel is calculated as follows:

	£
List price £15,000 × 19% (14% + (80 - 55)/5)	2,850
£2,850 × $^{10}/_{12}$	2,375
Less contribution (10 × £25)	(250)
	2,125
Fuel benefit £24,500 × 19% × $^{10}/_{12}$	3,879
Total taxable benefit	6,004

If the contribution of £25 per month had been towards the petrol, the contribution would not be deducted, making the benefit assessable £250 greater. Conversely, if the cost of private petrol was fully reimbursed by the employee, then there would have been no fuel benefit at all.

Activity 2: Car and fuel benefit

Damon who works for Stuart Ltd earns £52,500 (PAYE £21,000) and has use of a company car, a Jaguar S-Type 2.5 (brand new). The CO_2 emissions rate is 127 g/km and the car was first registered in December 2019. The car has a list price of £60,000 but the employer negotiated a discount and bought it for £57,000. The company fitted accessories (CD player and child safety seat) at a cost of £900.

Damon is required to pay £100 per month towards the running costs of the car (excluding petrol). The company meets all Damon's petrol costs in 2020/21 which amounted to £3,500.

Required

(a) What is Damon's taxable benefit for 2020/21?

£ [   ]

(b) What is the benefit if Damon left the company on 1 January 2021 and returned the car on that date?   £ [   ]

3.2 Vans

There is a £3,490 charge when vans are available to employees for private use.

Assessment focus point

Note that, unlike company cars, a home to work journey does not qualify as private use for a van.

If the van has CO_2 emissions of 0, then the benefit is 80% of the normal benefit, ie £2,792.

There is an additional £666 charge if fuel is made available for private use.

3.3 Other assets

The following rules apply if any other asset is provided to an employee.

3.3.1 Use of asset

Formula to learn

If an employee is allowed to use an asset owned by their employer for private purposes they will be assessed on the higher of:

*   20% of the value when first made available to employee
*   Rental paid by employer

3.3.2 Gift of asset

Formula to learn

If an employee is given an asset that previously belonged to their employer they will be assessed as follows:

*   If already used by employee, the higher of:
    -   Market value when given
    -   Original value when first used less values already assessed
*   If a new asset is given, then the employee will be assessed on the cost of providing the asset.
*   If the asset is a computer, the benefit can only be current market value.
*   Deduct from the benefit any payment the employee makes for the asset.

Illustration 4: Use and gift of asset

A suit costing £200 is bought by an employer for use by an employee on 6 April 2019. On 6 April 2020, the suit is purchased by the employee for £15, its market value then being £25.

The benefit taxable in 2019/20 will be 20% × £200 = £40

The benefit taxable in 2020/21 will be the greater of:

(a) Market value at acquisition by employee = £25

(b)

	£	£
Original market value	200	
Less assessed in respect of use 2019/20	(40)	
	160	
Therefore (b)		160
Less price paid by employee		(15)
Taxable benefit 2020/21		145

Activity 3: Use and gift of employer's asset

Gustav Holst, an employee, was given the use of some video equipment on 6 October 2018, when it had a value of £1,000. On 6 January 2021, he was given the asset outright when it was worth £500.

Required

Complete the following:

In 2020/21, his benefit for the use of the asset is £ _____

In 2020/21, his benefit on the gift of the asset is £ _____

3.4 Beneficial loans

There is a benefit when an employer gives an employee an interest-free loan or when the employer charges less than a commercial interest rate.

The benefit is the difference between the interest that should have been charged, using the official rate of interest (given in the exam), and the interest paid by the employee.

Formula to learn

Where the size of the loan has changed during the year, the interest is calculated on either of the following:

- The average loan outstanding in the year
- The loan outstanding on a month by month basis

The average method is usually used but either the taxpayer or HMRC can elect to use the month by month calculation.

There is no benefit if the total of all loans made to the employee in the year is £10,000 or less. If this limit is broken then all loans are taxed, not just the excess over £10,000.

An employee will always be taxed on the value of a loan written off by the employer even if the loan was below the £10,000 limit.

Illustration 5: Beneficial loan

At 6 April 2020, a low interest loan of £30,000 was outstanding to a director, who repaid £20,000 on 6 January 2021. The remaining balance of £10,000 was outstanding at 5 April 2021. Interest paid during the year was £250.

The benefit under both methods for 2020/21, assuming that the official rate of interest was 2.25% throughout 2020/21, is calculated as follows:

Average method

	£
$2^1/_4\% \times \dfrac{(30,000 + 10,000)}{2}$	450
Less interest paid	(250)
Taxable benefit	200

Alternative method

	£
$£30,000 \times {}^9/_{12} \times 2^1/_4\%$	506
(6 April 2020 – 6 January 2021)	
$£10,000 \times {}^3/_{12} \times 2^1/_4\%$	56
(7 January 2021 – 5 April 2021)	
	562
Less interest paid	(250)
Taxable benefit	312

Therefore, the taxable benefit will be £200.

Activity 4: Beneficial loan

At 6 April 2020, a taxable cheap loan of £40,000 was outstanding to an employee earning £12,000 a year, who repaid £25,000 on 7 July 2020. The remaining balance of £15,000 was outstanding at 5 April 2021. Interest paid during the year was £250.

Assume the official rate of interest was 2.25%.

Required

Complete the following sentences:

The benefit calculated under the average method is £ [   ]

The benefit calculated under the strict method is £ [   ]

The taxpayer would be taxed on £ [   ]

3.5 Accommodation

3.5.1 Job-related accommodation

An employee who is provided with **job-related accommodation** will not be taxed on it under the benefit rules.

Key term

Job-related accommodation is that which is:

- Provided for security reasons, for example for the Prime Minister;

- Necessary for the proper performance of duties, for example a caretaker; or

- Customary for that sort of work and ensures better performance of duties, for example a pub landlord would traditionally be provided with accommodation.

3.5.2 Accommodation that is not job related

If the accommodation is not job related, then a taxable benefit arises on employees and is calculated in two stages:

(1)   The basic charge is calculated as:

Formula to learn

Basic charge – greater of:

- Annual value
- Rent paid by employer

Illustration 6: Accommodation rented by employer

Tony is provided with a company flat:

	£
Annual value	3,000
Rent paid by the company	3,380
Amount paid by Tony to the company for the use of the flat	520

Tony's taxable benefit is:

	£
Benefit: greater of:	
(a) Annual value	3,000
(b) Rent paid by the company	3,380
Therefore	3,380
Less reimbursed to the company	(520)
Net benefit	2,860

(2)   There is an additional charge if the employer owns the building and the cost of the property is greater than £75,000. This is calculated as:

Formula to learn

Accommodation additional charge: (Cost – 75,000) × official rate of interest

Illustration 7: Accommodation owned by employer

Simon's employer provided him with a house throughout 2020/21. The company bought the house for £133,000 on 1 April 2015.

For 2020/21, the annual value of the house is £1,400. Simon pays £2,000 for the use of the house to his employer.

The total benefit arising in respect of the house for 2020/21, assuming the official rate of interest is 2.25%, is:

Basic charge:

	£
Annual value	1,400
Less Simon's contribution	(1,400)
	Nil

Additional charge:

	£	£
Cost	133,000	
Less	(75,000)	
Excess		58,000
£58,000 × 2.25%		1,305
Less Simon's contribution (£2,000 – 1,400)		(600)
Total benefit 2020/21		705

(3) If the accommodation was acquired more than six years before it was provided to an employee, then the additional charge is based on the market value at the start of the tax year in which the employee moves in.

Activity 5: Accommodation benefit

Ralph has the use of a house belonging to his employer, for which he pays a nominal rent of £2,500. The annual value is £3,000. Ralph has lived in the house since October 2000. It had cost the company £175,000 in October 1997 but was worth £300,000 when Ralph moved in.

Take the official rate of interest at 2.25%.

Required

(a) **What is the benefit if the accommodation is job related?**

£ [   ]

(b) **What is the benefit if the accommodation is not job related?**

£ [   ]

(c) **What is the benefit if the accommodation is not job related but was bought in October 1992?**

£ [   ]

3.5.3 Accommodation living expenses

A benefit arises on an employee if their household living expenses are paid for by their employer.

The benefit depends on the accommodation provided:

Formula to learn

- Job-related accommodation:

  Lower of

  – Cost of expenses to employer
  – 10% × net earnings (ie employment income including all other benefits)

- Not job related:

  – Cost of expenses to employer

Expenses include the following items:

- Heating, lighting, cleaning etc
- Repairing, maintaining or decorating
- Providing furniture (annual value taken as 20% of cost)

Activity 6: Accommodation living expenses

Maggie lives in accommodation provided by her employer and her salary is £7,000 per year. Household expenses of £1,800 are paid by her employer and she has other benefits totalling £2,000.

Required

Complete the following sentences:

If the property is 'job related' her benefit is   £ [   ]

If the property is not 'job related' her benefit is   £ [   ]

3.6 Vouchers

The employee is normally taxed on the cost incurred by the employer in providing a voucher or credit token (for example a credit card).

If the employee receives a cash voucher, a voucher that can be exchanged for cash, they are taxed on the amount that the voucher can be exchanged for.

Certain vouchers are exempt (see below).

4 Exempt benefits

The following benefits are not taxable. Much of this information is provided in the reference material and tax tables in the assessment.

(a)   Job-related accommodation.

(b)   Canteen offering free or discounted food available to all staff. A benefit would arise if the canteen was only available to selected staff members. The benefit would be the cost to the company net of payments made by the employee.

(c)   Qualifying removal expenses up to £8,000 when the employee has to move house because of their job. Qualifying costs include legal and removal costs as well as purchasing replacement goods such as curtains and carpets. Excess payments over the £8,000 would be taxable.

(d)   Car parking spaces near place of work.

(e)   Occasional taxi fares home where employees are required to work late after 9:00pm.

(f)   Use of pool cars.

(g)   Workplace nurseries (crèches). The crèche must be operated by the employer.

(h)   Contributions by an employer into an approved pension scheme.

(i)   Sport and recreational facilities available generally for the staff. These must be provided directly by the employer. If the employer pays for facilities provided by an external supplier then this will create a taxable benefit.

(j)   Outplacement counselling services to employees made redundant who have been employed full time for at least two years. The services can include counselling to help adjust to the loss of the job and to help in finding other work.

(k)   Annual staff events up to a maximum of £150 per head. If this limit is exceeded then the full cost is taxable.

(l)   Incidental expense of £5 per night if working away from home (telephone calls, laundry etc). The limit is £10 if working abroad. These amounts may be aggregated if working away a number of days; for example, if working away for three days then the limit for the period would be £15. If this limit is exceeded then the whole amount is taxable.

(m)   Mileage allowances (see later).

(n)   Mobile phones – these are exempt if a single phone is provided. A benefit would apply to additional phones provided to the employee.

(o)   £6 per week may be paid tax free to cover the cost of home working when the employee is required to work from home. Greater amounts may be claimed if the taxpayer can produce evidence of the actual costs incurred by working from home.

(p)   Subsidies paid to bus services used by employees for commuting.

(q)   Provision of buses for nine or more employees for commuting.

(r)   Provision of bicycles and cycling safety equipment for commuting.

(s)   Non-cash gifts given to employees as a reward for service in excess of 20 years are exempt provided the cost is no more than £50 per year worked.

(t)   Awards under staff suggestion schemes up to £5,000.

(u)   Air miles obtained by business travel.

(v)   Work-related training.

(w)   'Goodwill' gifts of up to £250 from a single third party.

(x)   Gifts made to employees outside of employment, for example a marriage gift.

5 Allowable deductions

Certain expenses may be deducted from employment income before tax is applied.

Assessment focus point

The general rule for allowable deductions states that expenses must be incurred **'wholly, exclusively and necessarily'** (HMRC, 2014) in the performance of duties. This means that if the employee could perform their duties without incurring the expense then it is not deductible as it is not strictly necessary.

The following are specific allowable deductions:

•   Fees and subscriptions to relevant professional bodies

•   Travelling and other expenses incurred in the performance of duties

- Contributions to an approved occupational pension scheme; an occupational scheme is one provided by the employer

- Donations to charity under **payroll deduction scheme**

5.1 Expenses

Employees will incur expenditure performing their job. They may or may not be reimbursed by their employer for these expenses. Certain business expenses are allowable:

- Wholly, exclusively and necessarily incurred in the performance of the duties of the employment;

- Qualifying travel expenses (see 5.1.4); or

- Professional fees and subscriptions.

The treatment of these expenses depends upon whether the employee is reimbursed for the expenditure by their employer or not.

5.1.1 Employee incurs expenditure without reimbursement

If the employee bears the cost of the expense themselves without reimbursement from their employer then they would simply deduct the expense from their employment income.

Illustration 8: Expenses not reimbursed

Paul earns a salary of £35,000 a year. He has to pay his £500 subscription to the Chartered Institute of Taxation. Paul's employer does not reimburse him for this expense.

Paul's employment income calculation would be as follows:

	£
Salary	35,000
Less expenses	(500)
Employment income	34,500

5.1.2 Employee incurs expenditure and is reimbursed by employer, or employer pays directly

Since 2016/17 the payment or reimbursement of expenses has been exempt (ie no need to include in earnings) if they are fully allowable and the employee would therefore otherwise be able to claim a deduction.

Illustration 9: Reimbursed expenses

Paul earns a salary of £35,000 a year. His employer reimburses him for his £500 subscription to the Chartered Institute of Taxation.

The subscription is exempt income as it is a reimbursed allowable expense, so it is not included in the calculations of earnings.

	£
Salary	35,000
Reimbursed expenses (exempt)	nil
Employment income	35,000

5.1.3 Expenses with a private and business element

Strictly, if an expense has a 'private' and 'business' component, then it is not exclusively used in the duties of employment and will not be allowed (for example if a phone is used for work purposes and privately, then no deduction can be claimed for the line rental, although the cost of the business calls would be allowed).

In practice, HMRC will allow taxpayers to apportion costs where there is a business and a private element. The business use will be an allowable expense, and deductible for the employee on their tax return. If the allowable element is clearly identifiable, the exemption will apply.

5.1.4 Travel expenses

Travelling expenses are deductible; if the employer reimburses this is an exempt benefit. As noted above, if expenses are not reimbursed then the taxpayer may deduct the expense.

Only business travelling is allowable. Normal commuting from home to office is not included.

An exception is where an employee is seconded to a **temporary workplace** for less than 24 months; here commuting from home is allowable.

5.1.5 Approved mileage allowance payments

Employers may reimburse employees for using their own car on their employer's business. The reimbursement is to cover fuel and all other costs associated with using the car, for example depreciation, road tax and insurance.

Formula provided

The allowable limits are:

- 45p per mile for the first 10,000 miles per tax year
- 25p per mile for the excess

If the employer pays more than the permitted amount, the excess is taxable.

If the employer pays less than the permitted amount, the employee can deduct the difference from their earnings.

There are separate rates for motorcycles and bicycles. These would be given to you in the exam.

Illustration 10: Statutory mileage

Owen drives 14,000 business miles in the tax year using his own car.

You are required to calculate the taxable benefit/allowable deduction assuming:

(a) He is reimbursed 45p a mile
(b) He is reimbursed 25p a mile

	£
Statutory limit: 10,000 × 45p	4,500
4,000 × 25p	1,000
	5,500

(a)

	£
Amount received (14,000 × 45p)	6,300
Less statutory limit	(5,500)
Taxable benefit	800

(b)

	£
Amount received (14,000 × 25p)	3,500
Less statutory limit	(5,500)
Allowable deduction	(2,000)

Activity 7: Statutory mileage

Jen drives 15,000 miles in the tax year.

Required

(a) Choose the correct option and insert the numerical value.

If Jen's employer pays her 30p per mile she

may deduct	is taxed on	£

(b) Choose the correct option and insert the numerical value.

If Jen's employer pays her 50p per mile, she

may deduct	is taxed on	£

5.1.6 Entertaining customers

If an employee spends money entertaining customers or clients and claims reimbursement, the normal rules seen above will apply.

Rather than reimbursing specific expenses, an employer may simply give an employee an annual allowance to cover expenses. As this is effectively additional salary, it is taxable but the employee may claim a deduction for expenses actually incurred.

The exception to this is that an employee may not claim a deduction against a round sum allowance for entertaining costs.

This is because the employer is claiming a deduction against their profits for paying the employee the allowance. Normally, a business cannot claim a deduction for entertaining costs. If the employee is allowed to escape taxation on this part of the allowance, then effectively customers are being entertained with no tax consequences for the employer or employee.

5.2 Contributing to a pension

An employee may save tax by paying into a pension.

5.2.1 Maximum contributions

Formula to learn

The maximum tax relief available for pension contributions each year is the higher of:

*   £3,600
*   Earnings for the year

Additional contributions are permitted but no tax relief will be available on these.

BPP
LEARNING MEDIA

5.2.2 Tax relief

Effectively the taxpayer's income is being reduced by the payment into the pension scheme so they are no longer paying tax on the top level of their income. They therefore save the tax they would have paid on this income. This saving may be at 20%, 40% or 45% depending on their level of income. A 20% taxpayer saves tax of 20p for every £1.00 contribution, a 40% taxpayer saves tax at 40p for every £1.00, while a 45% taxpayer would save 45p for every £1.00.

The method of relief is different depending on the type of pension scheme.

Key term

Personal pension scheme A personal pension scheme is organised by the taxpayer. Contributions are made net of basic rate tax (20%). As we saw in Chapter 2 - Calculation of Income Tax, additional relief is available for higher and additional rate taxpayers by **extending the basic and higher rate bands**.

Occupational scheme An occupational scheme is one provided by an employer. Contributions are deducted directly from earnings. PAYE is then applied to just the remaining income. This is called a **net pay arrangement**.

5.2.3 Employer contributions

An employer may also contribute to either an occupational scheme or a personal scheme on behalf of the employee.

Employer contributions are not taxable benefits on the employee.

There is no limit on the amount of contributions an employer can make.

5.3 Donations to charity

Employees may request that their employer pays some of their salary to an approved charity of their choice.

The donation is deducted from gross salary before PAYE is applied. It therefore saves the taxpayer tax at their highest marginal rate of tax.

This is sometimes called '**Give-As-You-Earn**' or **GAYE**.

6 Tax planning

There are a number of ways an employee can legally reduce their taxable income from employment:

(a)   Select exempt benefits over taxable benefits

(b)   Select benefits with a lower cash equivalent over benefits with a higher cash equivalent

(c)   Ensure that any contribution towards the private use of an employer's car is for the use itself as this would be deductible rather than for the private fuel which would not be deductible

(d)   Pay into a company pension scheme

(e) Make payments to charity under the payroll giving scheme

(f) Claim all allowable deductions, for example any travel costs of attending meetings at 'temporary workplaces'

(g) Avoid overtime working if this will take their income over £100,000 leading to a reduction in the personal allowance and a significant increase in tax (see Chapter 1)

(h) Seek rewards in benefits rather than in cash as there will be no National Insurance cost to the employee on benefits (note that the employer would have to pay National Insurance here)(see Chapter 5)

Chapter summary

- It is important to distinguish between income from employment and self-employment. The basic question is whether the person is employed under a contract of service, or performs services under a contract for services.

- An employee's earnings comprise wages or salary and bonuses and benefits.

- Money earnings are received on the earlier of the time payment is made and when the employee becomes entitled to payment. There are special rules for directors.

- The taxable benefit on a car is a percentage of the car's list price. This varies with carbon dioxide emissions/electric range, fuel type and the date the car was registered. There is an additional benefit if fuel is provided.

- The private use of a pool car is an exempt benefit.

- There is a taxable benefit for private use of a van (but home to work travel is not treated as private use) plus a further benefit if private fuel is provided.

- If the employer provides the employee with assets for private use, there is a taxable benefit each year of 20% of the value of the assets when first provided.

- Employer loans written off give rise to a taxable benefit. For loans there is a benefit equal to the excess of official rate of interest over interest actually charged.

- The living accommodation benefit is based on the annual value of the property. An additional benefit arises where the cost of the property exceeds £75,000.

- Expenses incurred by the employer in connection with the provision of living accommodation are fully assessable on the employee, unless the employee is in job-related accommodation in which case the benefit is restricted.

- There are certain exempt benefits which are not taxable for employees.

- A deduction is given to employees for using their own vehicle for business travel if any mileage allowance paid is less than the statutory rates. Any excess is taxable.

- Employees are generally allowed a deduction for travel costs incurred in the performance of their duties, or incurred in travelling to and from home to a temporary workplace. Temporary is taken to be not exceeding 24 months.

- Occupational pension schemes are employer-run schemes. No taxable benefit arises in respect of employer contributions made to pension schemes.

- Employee contributions to an occupational pension scheme are deducted from the employee's taxable earnings before tax is applied.

- Individuals can make pension contributions up to the higher of:
  - The basic limit (£3,600 – 2020/21)
  - Earnings for the year

- Employees can make charitable donations under an employer's payroll deduction scheme. Such payments are deductible in arriving at taxable earnings.

- For other employment-related expenses to be deductible, such expenses must be 'wholly, exclusively and necessarily' (HMRC, 2014) incurred 'in the performance of' the employee's duties.

Keywords

- **Approved mileage allowance payments scheme:** Lays down authorised mileage rates (AMR) at which employees may claim an allowance for business journeys made in their own car

- **Job-related accommodation:** Accommodation that is either necessary for the proper performance of duties, or for the better performance of the employee's duties and is customarily provided in that type of employment, or is provided as part of special security arrangements

- **Net pay arrangements:** Where an employer deducts an employee's occupational pension contributions from the employee's earnings before they deduct income tax

- **Payroll deduction scheme:** Set up by an employer to enable employees to make tax-deductible donations to charity

- **Temporary workplace:** One at which the employee expects to be for no more than 24 months

1 **Fill in the missing words.**

Someone is regarded as self-employed if they have a contract [   ],
whereas if they have a contract [   ], they will be regarded as an employee.

2 **Fill in the missing words.**

Expenses are allowable if they are incurred [   ], [   ] and
[   ] in the performance of the duties of employment.

3 Brian uses his own car to travel 8,000 business miles in the tax year. Brian's
employer reimburses him with 35p per mile travelled. The approved mileage rate
for the first 10,000 business miles travelled is 45p per mile.

**The amounts that are taxable(deductible) in calculating employment
income are (both minus signs and brackets can be used to indicate
negative numbers):**

£ [   ]

4 An employee is provided with a flat by his employer (not job-related
accommodation). The annual value of the flat is £4,000; rent paid by the employer
amounts to £5,900 per annum.

The taxable value of this benefit for the tax year is:

£ [   ]

5 A taxable fuel benefit is reduced by any reimbursement by the employee of the cost
of fuel provided for private mileage.

Tick ONE box.

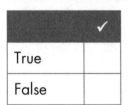

	✓
True	
False	

6 A video recorder costing £500 was made available to Gordon by his employer on 6 April 2019. On 6 April 2020, Gordon bought the recorder for £150, when its market value was £325.

The assessable benefit that arises in 2020/21 is:

	✓
£325	
£400	
£175	
£250	

7 There is no benefit on the first £10,000 of an interest-free loan.

Tick ONE box.

	✓
True	
False	

8 Gautown was supplied with a hybrid car by his employer throughout 2020/21 which was registered in January 2020. The list price of the car was £24,000, its CO_2 emissions were 38 g/km and its electric range was 50 miles.

The taxable benefit arising in respect of the car is:

£

9 Buster is the Managing Director of Buster Braces Ltd and is supplied with a Bentley (3 litre, petrol engine) which cost £72,000. It has CO_2 emissions of 138 g/km and was registered and provided to Buster on 6 April 2020. All running costs are borne by the company. Buster is also provided with a mobile phone for private and business use. The cost of provision of the phone to Buster Braces Ltd is £750 in 2020/21.

The total taxable benefits are:

£

10 **For each of the following benefits, tick whether they would be taxable or exempt if received by an employee in 2020/21:**

Item	Taxable	Exempt
Write off loan of £8,000 (only loan provided)		
Payments by employer of £500 per month into registered pension scheme		
Provision of one mobile phone		
Provision of a company car for both business and private use		
Removal costs of £5,000 paid to an employee relocating to another branch		
Accommodation provided to enable the employee to spend longer time in the office		

Property income

4

Learning outcomes

2	Calculate a UK taxpayer's total income
2.3	Calculate income from property
	• Calculate profit and losses from residential furnished and unfurnished property
3	Calculate income tax and National Insurance (NI) contributions payable by a UK taxpayer
3.5	Advise on tax planning techniques to minimise tax liabilities
	• Change investment incomes to make them more tax efficient

Assessment context

Task 5 in the initial AAT sample assessment tested the detailed rules on property income for 6 marks. Task 6 required you to produce a detailed income tax calculation for 12 marks and this included a brief working for property income. Task 8 consisted of a number of requirements for 7 marks, one of which tested tax planning for a couple with investment income.

Qualification context

You will not see these areas again in your AAT qualification outside of this unit.

Business context

Property may be an additional source of income for some people. For others, it will be their livelihood. Anyone investing in property needs to understand the tax implications.

Chapter overview

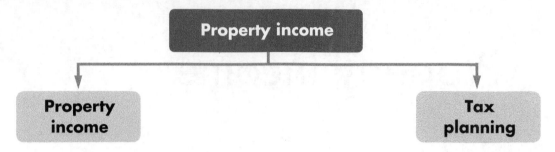

Property income

Property income

- Pool all UK rents
- If receipts ≤ £150,000 use cash basis
- If receipts > £150,000 use accruals basis
- Claim for replacement of furniture
- Relief for losses

Tax planning

- Transfer ownership of property to spouse/CP paying lower rate of tax

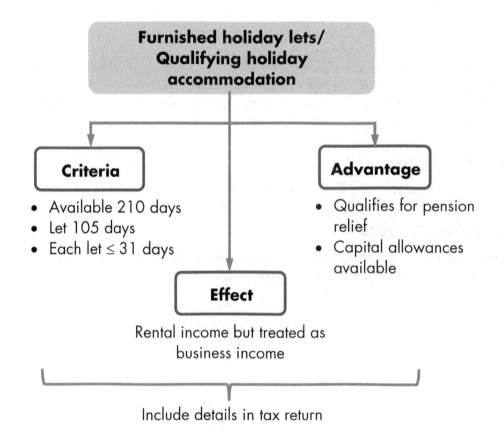

Furnished holiday lets/ Qualifying holiday accommodation

Criteria

- Available 210 days
- Let 105 days
- Each let ≤ 31 days

Advantage

- Qualifies for pension relief
- Capital allowances available

Effect

Rental income but treated as business income

Include details in tax return

Introduction

Before we can calculate income tax payable for the tax year we need to calculate a taxpayer's total income. This consists of the grand total of their income from various sources. One source of income included in this total would be the income realised from letting out property. This chapter looks at how we calculate this income.

1 Property income

1.1 What is property income?

Property income is all income derived from renting out land and/or buildings.

Key term

> **Landlord** The person letting out the property.
>
> **Tenant** The person letting the property.

1.2 Basis of assessment

A landlord normally uses the cash basis to calculate property income for the current tax year (although they can opt to use accruals basis if they wish).

Under the cash basis, property income = receipts – allowable expenses paid. This is taxed as non-savings income.

The exception to this rule is if the landlord receives > £150,000 in rents in one tax year, in which case they will have to use the accruals basis. Unless told otherwise you should assume the landlord receives ≤ £150,000 and uses the cash basis.

> **Illustration 1: Cash basis**
>
> Susie bought a property on 6 September 2020. She began letting the property immediately for an annual rent of £36,000 payable in advance in 3-monthly instalments due on 6 September, 6 December, 6 March and 6 June. Susie's tenant makes all rental payments on time.
>
> Rental income is taxed using the cash basis. This means the income which is received from the letting between 6 September 2020 and 5 April 2021 is taxed in 2020/21. During the tax year 2020/21 Susie receives £36,000 × $^3/_{12}$ ie £9,000 on 6 September 2020, 6 December 2020 and 6 March 2021 and is therefore taxed on £9,000 × 3 = £27,000.

1.3 Allowable deductions from property income

The landlord may deduct all incidental expenses, also calculated on a **cash basis,** ie only deducting those which have actually been paid. These must be revenue in nature, this means regular ongoing costs giving a short-term benefit, for example insurance. Capital costs are not deductible; these are one-off expenses that give a long-term benefit, for example installing central heating.

The following costs would be allowable if paid by the landlord:

- Advertising, accountancy and insurance

- Business rates and council tax

- Bad debts

- Management and agent's fees

- Fixed rate deductions for motor vehicles (using the approved mileage allowance rates seen in Chapter 3, Section 5.1.5)

1.4 Repair expenditure

Sometimes it is difficult to distinguish between revenue and capital expenses. A good example would be repair costs. If the costs constitute regular costs required to maintain the property in its current condition then these would be allowable, for example decorating and routine maintenance.

If the repair represents an improvement then it is not allowable, for example if the landlord installed a second bathroom in the property. Note also that if the building is bought in a dilapidated state then the initial costs incurred to make it usable again would also be capital and not allowed.

1.5 Furniture

There is no relief available when the landlord first buys furniture and equipment for the property.

When these assets are replaced the landlord may claim the full cost of the replacement in the tax year in which the replacements were bought.

The following assets would qualify for replacement furniture relief:

- Movable furniture or furnishings, such as beds or suites
- Televisions
- Fridges and freezers
- Carpets and floor coverings
- Curtains
- Linen
- Crockery or cutlery
- Beds and other furniture

If an asset is replaced with a better asset then only the cost of a similar replacement would be allowable.

Note that replacement of integral features such as bathrooms and central heating systems would be covered by the repair rules above.

1.6 Capital allowances

Capital allowances may be claimed on plant and machinery used in the letting business (you would be given a figure for this).

Illustration 2: Allowable expenses

Nadine has let a furnished property for many years. The rent received during 2020/21 is £41,000.

Expenses relating to the letting were:

	£
Insurance (year to 31 December 2020)	600
Insurance (year to 31 December 2021)	800

The insurance is paid monthly on the 1st of the month.

In June 2020, the tenant accidentally flooded the bathroom. Nadine took the opportunity to strip out the aged bathroom suite and convert the bathroom into a wet room at a total cost of £5,000. This included £900 that was the cost of repairing the flood damage.

During the year the washing machine broke and Nadine bought a replacement washer/drier for £400. An equivalent washing machine would have cost £300.

Nadine's property income for 2020/21 is:

	£	£
Rental income		41,000
Less insurance (£600 × $^8/_{12}$) + (£800 × $^4/_{12}$)	667	
(paid 1 May → 1 Dec) (paid 1 Jan → 1 Apr)		
Replacement furniture relief at cost	300	
Repairs	900	
		(1,867)
Taxable property income		39,133

> **Note.** The rental income and expenses must be dealt with on a cash received and paid basis.
>
> The cost of the flood repairs is allowable because it is a revenue expense. However, the cost of converting the bathroom into a wet room is not allowable because this is a capital expense.

1.7 Accruals basis

To recap:

- a landlord in receipt of > £150,000 of rental income **cannot** use the cash basis and

- any landlord in receipt of ≤ £150,000 may opt out of the cash basis.

In this case they would instead use the accruals basis, whereby: property income = accrued income − accrued allowable expenses.

1.8 More than one property – pooling income and expenses

Income and expenses from different properties are pooled to give a single total for property income.

	£
Total property income received	X
Total allowable deductions paid	(X)
Profit/(loss)	X/(X)

Profits and losses on different properties are thus automatically offset.

> **Illustration 3: Property pooling calculation**
>
> Bahrat lets two properties in 2020/21.
>
> Property 1 was bought in June 2020 and let unfurnished from 1 July 2020 at an annual rent of £18,000 per annum, payable monthly on the first of the month. Buildings insurance of £9,000 was paid for the year to 30 June 2021. This was payable on a quarterly basis from 1 July 2020 onwards. £1,200 was spent in June 2020 on advertising for tenants.
>
> Property 2 became vacant on 5 April 2020. Bahrat then spent £7,500 on repairing the leaking roof in the property. The unfurnished property was let again with effect from 1 March 2021 for £24,000 per annum, payable monthly in advance. Buildings insurance of £1,800 was paid on 6 April 2020 for the year to 31 March 2021.

Bahrat's property income for 2020/21 is:

	£	£
Rental income – Property 1		
(10/12 × £18,000) (1 July → 1 Apr)		15,000
Rental income – Property 2		
(2/12 × £24,000)		4,000
Less: Buildings insurance		
– Property 1 (1 July, Oct, Jan, Apr)	9,000	
– Property 2	1,800	
Advertising for tenants	1,200	
Repairs	7,500	
		(19,500)
Overall property loss		(500)

Pooling income and expenses on all let properties effectively allows a loss on one property to be set against income from other properties.

1.9 Losses

If the overall result is a profit it is taxable in the current year.

If the overall result is a loss, carry it forward to use against property income in the future. The loss can carry forward indefinitely until it is used.

Activity 1: Property income

Fiona owns a property that she lets furnished on a short-term basis. In the year ended 5 April 2021, she received rents of £8,400 and incurred the following expenses:

	£
Agent's commission	360
Redecoration	500
Insurance paid on the last day of the month	
– year to 31 December 2020	400
– year to 31 December 2021	500
Repairs	1,200

Repairs include £300 to replace a broken window; the balance was to install a brand new window. There had been no window here before but Fiona decided the new window would offer views that would encourage future lettings.

She also replaced a single bed with a double bed. The double bed cost £400. An equivalent single bed would have cost £300.

Fiona has a property loss brought forward of £500.

Required

How much is assessable on her as property income in 2020/21?

£ _____

---

2 Property allowance

If gross receipts from property ≤ £1,000

- this income is automatically exempt due to the property allowance, unless

- the taxpayer elects to disapply the property allowance in which case they calculate the property income as normal: ie receipts – allowable expenses paid

If gross receipts from property > £1,000

- the taxpayer calculates the property income as normal: ie receipts – allowable expenses unless

- they elect to apply the property allowance, in which case they calculate the property income as receipts – £1,000

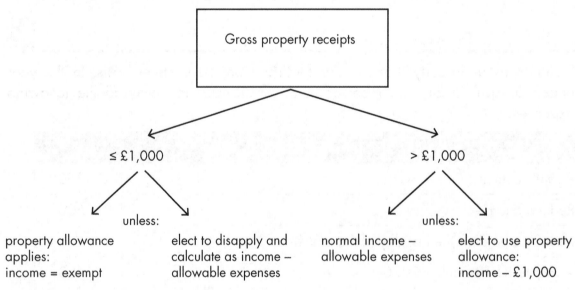

In either case the deadline for an election is the first anniversary of the 31 January following the tax year for which the election is being made.

Eg the deadline for an election for tax year 2020/21 is 31 January 2023.

Activity 2: Property allowance

Charlotte lets out her flat for £800 when she goes away on holiday and incurs expenses of:

(a)   £200

(b)   £900 due to extensive damage caused by the tenants.

Thomas lets out his house when he is seconded to another office for a month. He receives £1,500 of income and incurs advertising and cleaning expenses of:

(a)   £300

(b)   £1,050.

Required

Advise Charlotte and Thomas as to whether or not they should make an election and how much rental income they will be taxed on in each scenario.

3 Furnished holiday lets

Key term

Furnished holiday let   A furnished holiday let is a specific type of property that gives certain tax advantages to the landlord.

This can also be known as qualifying holiday accommodation.

Property income, net of expenses, is not pooled with that of the taxpayer's other lets.

Accommodation counts as a furnished holiday let (FHL) if it is:

(a)   Situated in the UK or in the European Economic Area

(b)   Furnished

(c)   Available for commercial letting to the public for not less than 210 days each tax year

(d)   Actually let for at least 105 days in each tax year

(e)   Holiday tenants should not stay for a period of more than 31 days; however, the property can be let to the same tenant for periods longer than this, provided these long lets do not take up more than 155 days per tax year

FHL accommodation income is taxable as property income but it is treated as a business.

Keep details of income and expenses separate to other properties.

The advantages of having an FHL are that:

(a) The income may be put in a pension scheme and tax relief claimed. Effectively no tax is paid on income placed in a pension scheme. No tax relief is available from normal rental income.

(b) Capital allowances are claimed on furniture rather than replacement furniture relief. This is usually more beneficial.

All UK FHL income is treated as a single business separate to other rental income.

Net losses from a UK FHL business may only be carried forward and offset against future UK FHL income; they cannot be offset against normal property income. Therefore it is important to **keep details of income and expenses separate from other properties**.

4 Tax planning

Property income is **non-savings** income and is taxed at 20%, 40% or 45% depending on the taxpayer's level of income.

Spouses or civil partners or couples cohabiting or friends or relatives may own property either jointly or individually. One party may be paying tax at a higher rate than the other. If this is the case it makes sense to have the property owned by the taxpayer who is paying tax at the lower rate as they will then receive the income and it will be taxed at a lower rate reducing the overall tax liability.

One party may therefore need to transfer property to another.

If one of the parties has no income then the property should be transferred to them so they can offset their personal allowance against the income. This will enable them to use a personal allowance that would otherwise have been wasted.

Assets including cash can be transferred between spouses and civil partners without causing inheritance tax or capital gains tax problems. If the parties are not married or in a civil partnership it may cause tax issues. For the planning to be effective the asset or cash to buy an asset must be transferred with 'no strings attached', the spouse receiving the asset has total control over it and makes no promises to return the asset at a later date or pay the income generated to the other party. Clearly you must trust the other party before following this course of action!

HMRC will disregard transactions which appear to be artificial and undertaken purely for a tax advantage so for the planning to work there must be some other purpose for the transaction, for example a wife with a husband who is not working could gift a property to him so that he has a source of income of his own and some independence.

Chapter summary

- Property income is all income derived from letting out land and buildings.

- It is calculated on a cash basis for a tax year and taxed as non-savings income.

- Expenditure is allowable if it is for regular ongoing costs, repairs or the replacement of furniture. Capital costs are not allowable.

- Income and expenses on different properties are pooled to give a grand total. A net positive result will be taxable. A net negative result is a loss that may be carried forward and offset against property income in the future.

- Income from qualifying holiday accommodation counts as earnings for pension purposes.

- Capital allowances may be claimed on furniture in qualifying holiday accommodation.

- Couples should ensure properties are owned by the spouse/civil partner who is paying tax at a lower rate or has an unused personal allowance.

Keywords

- **Accruals basis:** For taxing rental income means that all rent owing or accruing in a tax year is taxed in that year

- **Landlord:** Someone who rents out a property to another person

- **Tenant:** The person who occupies the land or building

Test your learning

1   David buys a property for letting on 1 August 2020 and grants a tenancy to Ethel from 1 December 2020 at £3,600 per annum, payable quarterly in advance.

   The rental income taxable in 2020/21 is:

   £ [   ]

2   John pays buildings insurance premiums for 12 months in advance on 1 October each year to cover all his rental properties. He pays £4,800 in 2019 and £5,200 in 2020.

   What amount for building insurance would be allowed against his rental income for 2020/21?

   £ [   ]

3   Harry owns a property which he lets for the first time on 1 July 2020 at a rent of £4,000 per annum, payable monthly in advance.

   The first tenants left on 28 February 2021 and the property was re-let to new tenants on 4 April 2021 at a rent of £5,000 per annum, payable yearly in advance.

   Harry's allowable expenditure was £1,000 in 2020/21.

   What is his taxable rental income for 2020/21?

   £ [   ]

4   Ben and Polly are married. Polly earns a salary of £200,000 a year meaning she pays tax at 45%, Ben has trading income of £20,000 meaning he pays tax at 20%. They are planning to buy an investment property which they will let out for £12,000 a year.

   To minimise their tax liability the property should be [▼]

   Picklist:

   held in Ben's name
   held in Polly's name
   held in trust
   held jointly by Ben and Polly

5   **Property losses may be:**

	✓
Carried back one year and offset against property income only	
Offset against net income in the current year	
Carried forward for one year only and offset against property income	
Carried forward indefinitely and offset against property income only	

National Insurance

5

Learning outcomes

3	Calculate income tax and National Insurance (NI) contributions payable by a UK taxpayer
3.4	Calculate NI contributions for employees and employers
	• Identify taxpayers who need to pay NI
	• Calculate NI contributions payable by employees
	• Calculate NI contributions payable by employers

Assessment context

Task 7 in the initial AAT sample assessment tested the calculation of Class 1 Employee, Class 1 Employer and Class 1A (employer) National Insurance for 4 marks.

Qualification context

You will not see the information in this chapter outside of this unit.

Business context

National Insurance is a significant extra cost for an employer and an employee. An employer will have to consider the National Insurance cost when taking on new staff or offering increased salary or benefits to existing staff.

Chapter overview

National Insurance

Class 1

- On cash earnings
- Exclude reimbursed expenses
- Include excessive mileage payments > 45p/mile
- Calculate weekly or monthly
- Annual calculation for directors

Class 1A

- Payable by employer
- On benefits
- Rate 13.8%

Employee

- Cost to employee
- £1–£9,500   0%
- £9,500–£50,000   12%
- £50,001 and above 2%

Employer

- Cost to employer
- £1–£8,788   0%
- £8,788 and above 13.8%
- Deduct employment allowance of £4,000 from total bill

Introduction

An employer will have to deduct **Class 1 Employee National Insurance** from their employees' cash earnings and pay this over to HMRC. This is a cost to the employee. In addition to this employers will have to pay over **Class 1 Employer National Insurance** on the employees' cash earnings as well as **Class 1A National Insurance** on non-cash benefits received by the employee (for example use of a car owned by the company). Both of these represent an additional cost to the employer. National Insurance contributions are sometimes abbreviated to NIC.

1 Class 1 Employee National Insurance

Key term

Class 1 Employee National Insurance This is deducted by the employer from the employees' earnings. It thus represents a cost to the employee.

1.1 What are earnings?

'Earnings' broadly comprise gross cash payments, excluding benefits which cannot be turned into cash by surrender (eg annual leave entitlement). **Certain payments are exempt.** In general the income tax and NIC exemptions mirror one another so if a payment is exempt for income tax it is also exempt for National Insurance. We considered exempt payments in detail in Chapter 3; for example if an employee works away from home their employer can pay them up to £5 a night to cover incidental expenses and these payments would not be chargeable to income tax or National Insurance.

An expense with a business purpose is not treated as earnings. For example, if an employee is reimbursed for business travel or for staying in a hotel on the employer's business this is not normally 'earnings'.

In general, vouchers are subject to Class 1 Employee and Employer as they are deemed to be a cash equivalent. For exempt vouchers see Chapter 3.

1.2 Rates of contributions

The rates of contribution for 2020/21, and the income bands to which they apply, are provided in the assessment and set out in the *Reference material and tax tables* section at the end of this Course Book.

Employees pay Class 1 employee's contributions at 12% of earnings between the employee's threshold of £9,500 and the upper earnings limit (UEL) of £50,000 or the equivalent monthly or weekly limit (see below). They also pay additional Class 1 employee's contributions of 2% on earnings above the upper earnings limit.

Illustration 1: Class 1 Employee National Insurance

Sally works for Red plc. She is paid £5,000 per month. Show Sally's Class 1 employee contributions deducted by Red plc for 2020/21.

Annual salary £5,000 × 12 = £60,000

Employee contributions	£
£(50,000 – 9,500) = £40,500 × 12% (main)	4,860
£(60,000 – 50,000) = £10,000 × 2% (additional)	200
Total employee contributions	5,060

Activity 1: Class 1 Employee National Insurance

Tyrone is one of 3,000 employees of Taverner plc.

	£
Salary for 2020/21	52,500
Non-cash benefits	6,450

Required

What amount of national insurance does Tyrone suffer in the tax year?

£ _____

2 Class 1 Employer National Insurance

Key term

Class 1 Employer National Insurance This is paid by the employer on top of the employees' earnings. It thus represents a cost to the employer.

2.1 What are earnings?

We use the same figure we calculated for the Employee calculation above.

2.2 Rates of contributions

The rates of contribution for 2020/21, and the income bands to which they apply, are provided in the assessment and set out in the *Reference material and tax tables* section at the end of this Course Book.

Employers pay contributions of 13.8% on earnings above the employer's threshold of £8,788, or the equivalent monthly or weekly limit. There is no upper limit.

Illustration 2: Class 1 Employer National Insurance

Sally works for Red plc. She is paid £5,000 per month.

Show Sally's employer contributions paid by Red plc for 2020/21.

Annual salary £5,000 × 12 = £60,000

Employer's threshold £8,788

Red plc	£
Employer contributions	
£(60,000 – 8,788) = £51,212 × 13.8%	7,067

Activity 2: Class 1 Employer National Insurance

Tyrone is one of 3,000 employees of Taverner plc.

	£
Salary for 2020/21	52,500
Non-cash benefits	6,450

Required

What amount of Class 1 employer national insurance does Tyrone's employer pay in the tax year?

£	

---

3 Earnings periods for Class 1 Employee and Employer National Insurance

In practice National Insurance is calculated with reference to the employee's earnings period so an employee who is paid weekly will have their National Insurance calculated using weekly thresholds and an employee who is paid monthly will have their National Insurance calculated using the monthly thresholds.

	Weekly £	Monthly £	Annual £
Employee's thresholds	183	792	9,500
Upper Earnings Limit (UEL)	962	4,167	50,000
Employer's thresholds	169	732	8,788

If the employee earns the same amount every week/month then the annual calculation we have previously calculated will yield the same result as the calculation based on the actual earnings period. If the employee earns different amounts in different periods then the annual calculation shortcut will not always give the correct result.

In your assessment you will probably have to perform an annual calculation unless you are instructed to do otherwise.

Directors have a greater degree of control over how they are paid than most employees. There is therefore a risk that they could manipulate the way they are paid to minimise their liability. To prevent this, their National Insurance is always calculated on a cumulative basis. The detail of this calculation is outside the scope of your studies but effectively it will yield the same result as the annual calculation.

Illustration 3: Earning periods for directors and other employees

Bill and Ben work for Weed Ltd. Bill is a monthly paid employee. Ben who is a director of Weed Ltd, is also paid monthly. Each is paid an annual salary of £45,900 in 2020/21 and each also received a bonus of £3,000 in December 2020.

Show the employee and employer contributions for both Bill and Ben, using a monthly earnings period for Bill. Ignore the employment allowance (see next section).

Bill

Regular monthly earnings £45,900/12 = £3,825

Employee contributions

	£
11 months	
£(3,825 – 792) = £3,033 × 12% × 11 (main only)	4,004
1 month (December)	
£(4,167 – 792) = £3,375 × 12% (main)	405
£(3,825 + 3,000 – 4,167) = £2,658 × 2% (additional)	53
Total employee contributions	4,462

Employer contributions

	£
11 months	
£(3,825 − 732) = £3,093 × 13.8% × 11	4,695
1 month (December)	
£(3,825 + 3,000 − 732) = £6,093 × 13.8%	841
Total employer contributions	5,536

Ben

Total earnings £(45,900 + 3,000) = £48,900

Employee contributions

	£
Total earnings do not exceed UEL	
£(48,900 − 9,500) = £39,400 × 12% (main)	4,728

Employer contributions

	£
£(48,900 − 8,788) = £40,112 × 13.8%	5,535

Because Ben is a director an annual earnings period applies. The effect of this is that increased employee contributions are due.

4 The employment allowance

An employer can make a claim to **reduce its total Class 1 employer contributions** by an **employment allowance equal to those contributions**, subject to a **maximum allowance of £4,000 per tax year**.

Some employers are **excluded employers** for the purposes of the employment allowance. These include those who employ **employees for personal, household or domestic work, public authorities** and employers who **carry out functions either wholly or mainly of a public nature** such as provision of National Health Service services. Companies where the director is the only employee are also excluded from the employment allowance.

In addition, the employment allowance is only available to employers with a total employers' Class 1 NIC liability **below £100,000 in the tax year before the claim**. If this information is not given in the exam, **assume that the employment allowance is available**.

Illustration 4: The employment allowance

Blue plc is a trading company which has two employees, one who earns £20,000 per year and the other who earns £30,000 per year. Each employee is paid in equal monthly amounts and so an annual computation of Class 1 can be made.

Calculate the Class 1 employer contributions payable by Blue plc for 2020/21.

	£
Employee 1: £(20,000 – 8,788) = 11,212 × 13.8%	1,547
Employee 2: £(30,000 – 8,788) = 21,212 × 13.8%	2,927
	4,474
Less employment allowance (maximum)	(4,000)
Employer contributions 2020/21	474

Activity 3: The employment allowance

Stoney Heap Ltd is a trading company which has two employees, one earns £18,000 per year and the other earns £15,000 per year. Each employee is paid in equal monthly amounts.

Required

How much Class 1 employer contributions are payable by Stoney Heap Ltd for 2020/21?

£ [ ]

5 Class 1A National Insurance

Key term

Class 1A National Insurance This is paid by the employer on the cash value of employees' non-cash benefits. It is paid in addition to the benefits. It thus represents a cost to the employer.

5.1 What are benefits?

If an employee is provided with non-cash benefits such as the use of a car belonging to the employer then we must calculate a cash equivalent value so that income tax and National Insurance may be applied. The calculation of the cash equivalent value is addressed in Chapter 3.

Assessment focus point

In National Insurance questions you will probably be given the value of the benefit although you may be expected to apply the rules in Chapter 3 to calculate it.

5.2 Rates of contributions

The rates of contribution for 2020/21 are provided in the assessment and set out in the *Reference material and tax tables* section of this Course Book.

We simply apply 13.8% to the cash value of the benefits.

Illustration 5: Class 1A National Insurance

Sally has the following benefits for income tax purposes.

	£
Company car	5,200
Living accommodation	10,000
Medical insurance	800

Calculate the Class 1A NICs that the employer will have to pay.

Total benefits are £16,000 (£10,000 + £5,200 + £800)

Class 1A NICs:

£16,000 × 13.8% = <u>£2,208</u>

Activity 4: Class 1A National Insurance

Tyrone is one of 3,000 employees of Taverner plc.

	£
Salary for 2020/21	52,500
Non-cash benefits	6,450

Required

The Class 1A National Insurance payable by Taverner plc is

£ [   ]

6 Reimbursed expenses including business mileage

As noted above, reimbursement of genuine expenses incurred in doing your job are not subject to Class 1 National Insurance.

However, if the employer was paying for a private expense of the employee it would be subject to National Insurance. For example if the employer reimbursed the employee for specific business phone calls National Insurance would not apply. If the employer paid for all of the employee's calls Class 1 Employee and Employer would be applied to the cost of the private calls reimbursed.

An employee may use their own car on their employer's business and be reimbursed for the cost incurred. The employer may reimburse up to 45p a mile without any National Insurance implications. Any sums paid in excess of 45p would be subject to Class 1 Employee and Employer National Insurance. Note this is slightly different from the income tax treatment we saw in Chapter 3 where a lower rate applies after 10,000 miles have been driven in a tax year.

Illustration 6: Business mileage

Sophie uses her own car for business travel. During the tax year, Sophie drove 15,400 miles in the performance of her duties. Sophie's employer paid her a mileage allowance. How is the mileage allowance treated for National Insurance purposes assuming that the rate paid is:

(a)   40p a mile?
(b)   50p a mile?

(a)

	£
Mileage allowance received (15,400 × 40p)	6,160
Permitted payment (15,400 × 45p)	(6,930)
Excess over limit	0

As the payment is within the permitted amount there is no charge to National Insurance.

(b)

	£
Mileage allowance received (15,400 × 50p)	7,700
Less tax-free amount (above)	(6,930)
	770

As the payment is above the permitted amount the excess of £770 will be chargeable to Class 1 National Insurance, Employee and Employer.

7 Tax planning

An employee may choose to receive non-cash benefits rather than a cash pay rise as cash earnings would be subject to Class 1 Employee whereas benefits would not be. The employer would probably be indifferent here between providing cash and benefits, as cash would be subject to Class 1 Employer whereas benefits would be subject to Class 1A, both at 13.8%.

- Class 1 National Insurance is applied to an employee's cash earnings from employment. Vouchers are included but reimbursed business expenses are excluded.

- Class 1 employee contributions are deducted from an employee's earnings. It is therefore a cost to the employee.

- Class 1 employer contributions are paid in addition to an employee's earnings. It is therefore a cost to the employer.

- Class 1 employee and employer are usually calculated with reference to an employee's earnings period, weekly or monthly. If the employee earns the same amount each period an annual shortcut calculation can be done instead.

- Directors will have their NIC calculated on a cumulative basis meaning that the annual calculation will always give the correct result.

- An employer is allowed to deduct the employment allowance from the Class 1 Employer's liability reducing the cost to them.

- Class 1A is payable by the employer on the cash equivalent value of non-cash benefits received by the employee.

- There is no Class 1 on the reimbursement of genuine business expenses but if the employer pays a private expense of the employee it will be subject to National Insurance. This includes excessive payments to an employee for the use of their own car.

Keywords

- **Class 1 Employee National Insurance:** The National Insurance deducted from an employee's earnings

- **Class 1 Employer National Insurance:** The National Insurance an employer pays on top of an employee's earnings

- **Class 1A National Insurance (employer):** The National Insurance an employer pays on the value of non-cash benefits received by an employee

- **Employment allowance:** An amount that can be deducted from the employer's Class 1 Employer's liability

1 Robert is one of 3,000 employees of George plc. He receives the following from his employer in tax year 2020/21:

	£
Salary	42,000
Reimbursed business expenses	3,000
Non-cash benefits	8,000

What amount of Class 1 Employee National Insurance contributions does Robert's employer pay over on his behalf? £ [ ]

What amount of Class 1 Employer National Insurance contributions does

Robert's employer pay in the tax year? £ [ ]

What amount of Class 1A National Insurance contributions does

Robert's employer pay in the tax year? £ [ ]

2 Alec works for Knight Ltd. He is paid monthly and receives an annual salary of £36,000 in 2020/21. He also receives a bonus of £10,000 in March 2021.

Show the Employee and Employer contributions for Alec using a monthly earnings period. Ignore the employment allowance.

Alec's Employee contributions are £ [ ]

Alec's Employer contributions are £ [ ]

3 Elizabeth is a director of Faerie plc. She is paid monthly and receives an annual salary of £49,000 in 2020/21 and receives a bonus of £10,000 in March 2021.

Show the Employee and Employer contributions for Elizabeth. Ignore the employment allowance.

Elizabeth's Employee contributions are £ [ ]

Elizabeth's Employer contributions are £ [ ]

4   Ursa Minor Beta plc is a trading company which has two employees, one earns £25,000 per year and the other who earns £60,000 per year. Each employee is paid in equal monthly amounts.

The Class 1 Employer contributions payable by Ursa Minor Beta plc

are £ [   ]

5   Toby uses his own car for business travel. During the tax year, Toby drove 18,500 miles in the performance of his duties. Toby's employer paid him a mileage allowance.

If the mileage allowance is 35p a mile the amount subject to Class 1

National Insurance is £ [   ]

If the mileage allowance is 50p a mile the amount subject to Class 1

National Insurance is £ [   ]

Chargeable gains

6

Learning outcomes

1	**Analyse the theories, principles and rules that underpin taxation systems**
1.4	**Discuss residence and domicile**
	• The definitions of residence and domicile
	• The impact that each of these has on the taxation position of a UK taxpayer
4	**Account for capital gains tax**
4.1	**Discuss chargeable and exempt capital transactions**
	• Chargeable and exempt assets
	• Chargeable and exempt persons
	• Connected persons
4.2	**Calculate chargeable gains and allowable losses**
	• Calculate chargeable gains and allowable losses on normal capital disposals (including compensation: assets damaged/destroyed)
	• Apply part disposals rules
	• Apply chattels and wasting chattel rules
4.4	**Calculate capital gains tax payable**
	• Apply current exemptions
	• Treat capital losses
	• Apply rates of capital gains tax
	• Identify the date on which capital gains tax is due

Assessment context

Task 9 of the initial AAT sample assessment required the calculation of chargeable gains for a number of different disposals testing a variety of the different rules in this chapter including those for chattels, exempt assets and connected parties, 10 marks were available. Task 11 required you to calculate the capital gains tax payable for a number of different taxpayers in different circumstances, 7 marks were available.

Qualification context

You will not see the information in this chapter outside of this unit unless you are also studying *Business Tax*.

Business context

People sell assets for a variety of reasons. It is important to realise when a charge to capital gains tax arises and when capital gains tax needs to be paid if a taxpayer is to avoid paying interest and penalties.

Chapter overview

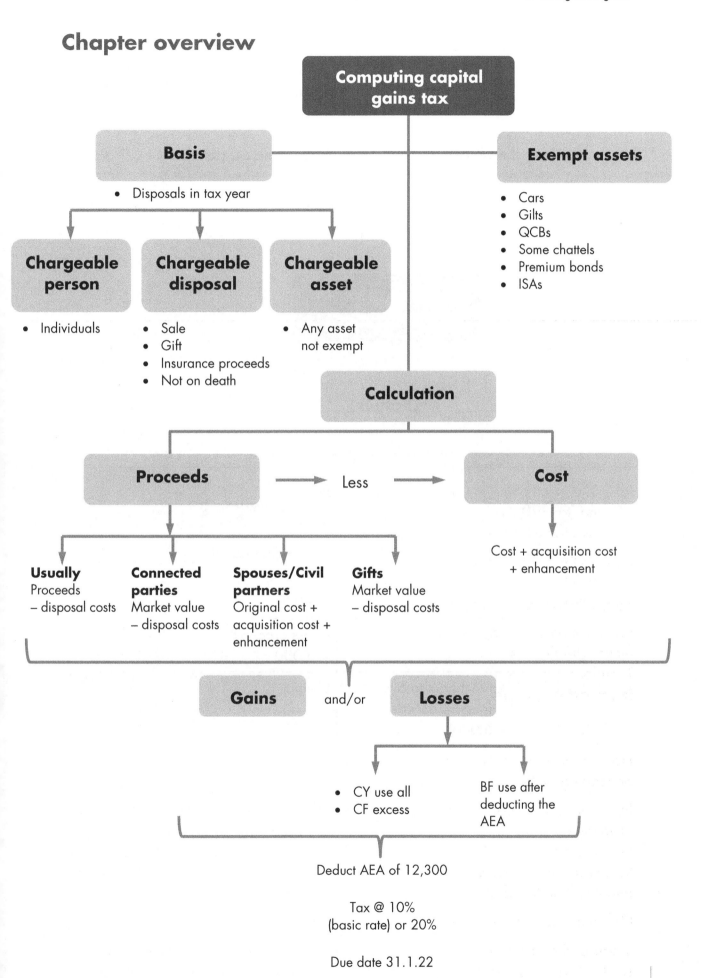

Computing capital gains tax

Basis
- Disposals in tax year

Chargeable person
- Individuals

Chargeable disposal
- Sale
- Gift
- Insurance proceeds
- Not on death

Chargeable asset
- Any asset not exempt

Exempt assets
- Cars
- Gilts
- QCBs
- Some chattels
- Premium bonds
- ISAs

Calculation

Proceeds → Less → **Cost**

Usually
Proceeds
– disposal costs

Connected parties
Market value
– disposal costs

Spouses/Civil partners
Original cost +
acquisition cost +
enhancement

Gifts
Market value
– disposal costs

Cost + acquisition cost
+ enhancement

Gains and/or **Losses**

- CY use all
- CF excess

BF use after
deducting the
AEA

Deduct AEA of 12,300

Tax @ 10%
(basic rate) or 20%

Due date 31.1.22

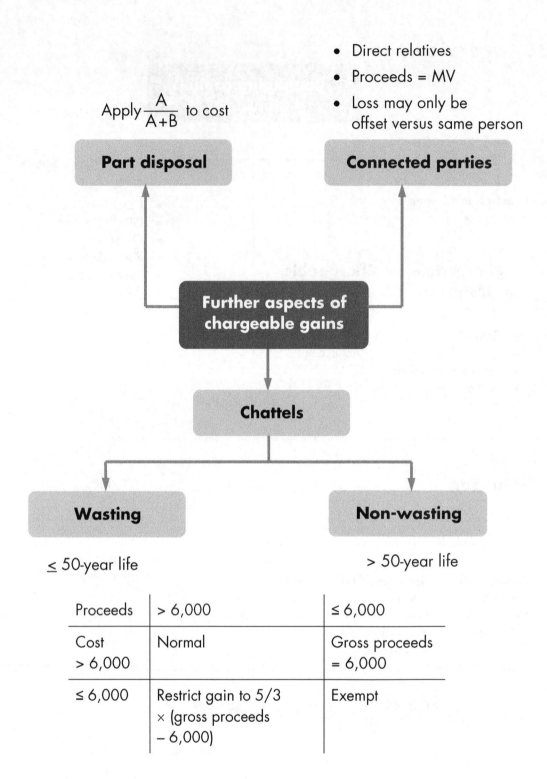

Apply $\dfrac{A}{A+B}$ to cost

Part disposal

- Direct relatives
- Proceeds = MV
- Loss may only be offset versus same person

Connected parties

Further aspects of chargeable gains

Chattels

Wasting

≤ 50-year life

Non-wasting

> 50-year life

Proceeds	> 6,000	≤ 6,000
Cost > 6,000	Normal	Gross proceeds = 6,000
≤ 6,000	Restrict gain to 5/3 × (gross proceeds − 6,000)	Exempt

Introduction

Income is a regular receipt that is expected to recur. A gain is a one-off disposal of a capital item.

Individuals pay **income tax** on income and **capital gains tax** on capital gains.

1 When does a chargeable gain arise?

For a disposable to be taxable there must be a **chargeable disposal** of a **chargeable asset** by a **chargeable person**.

1.1 Chargeable person

Individuals are chargeable persons.

1.2 Chargeable disposal

An individual is taxed on gains arising from disposals in the current tax year.

The following are the most important **chargeable disposals**:

- Sales of assets or parts of assets
- Gifts of assets or parts of assets
- The loss or destruction of an asset

A chargeable disposal occurs on the date of the contract (where there is one, whether written or oral), or the date of a conditional contract becoming unconditional.

Exempt disposals include:

- Transfers on death
- Gifts to charities

On death the heirs inherit assets as if they bought them at death for their then market values. There is no capital gain or allowable loss on death.

1.3 Chargeable assets

All assets are chargeable unless they are classified as exempt. The following are exempt:

- Motor vehicles suitable for private use
- UK government stocks (gilt-edged securities)
- Qualifying corporate bonds (company loan stock)
- **Wasting chattels** (greyhounds, racehorses) (see later)
- Premium bonds
- Investments held in an ISA

Assessment focus point

Make sure you identify an exempt asset, state that it is exempt in the exam and do not tax it.

2 Calculation of chargeable gains and allowable losses

Illustration 1: Basic capital gains computation

	£
Disposal consideration (or market value)	X
Less incidental costs of disposal	(X)
Net proceeds	X
Less allowable cost (including acquisition cost)	(X)
Less enhancement expenditure	(X)
Capital gain/(capital loss)	X/(X)

We now look at each of the items in the above proforma in turn.

2.1 Disposal consideration

Usually this is proceeds received. Note, though, that a disposal is deemed to take place at market value when the disposal is:

- A gift
- Made for a consideration that cannot be valued
- Deliberately sold for a consideration of less than market value
- Made to a connected person (see later)

Note that if a taxpayer makes a sale to an unconnected person and strikes a bad bargain then the actual proceeds achieved will be used. Market value is only used for a sale between unconnected persons when the taxpayer deliberately chooses to sell at undervalue to give the buyer a benefit.

Where a chargeable asset is lost or destroyed the taxpayer may receive insurance money as compensation for their loss. In that case the loss/destruction is treated as a chargeable disposal, with the money received from the insurance company being the disposal proceeds.

2.2 Costs

The following costs are deducted in the above proforma:

(a) **Incidental costs of disposal**

These are the costs of selling an asset. They may include advertising costs, estate agents' fees, legal costs and valuation fees. These costs should be deducted separately from any other allowable costs.

(b) **Allowable costs**

These include:

(i) The original purchase price of the asset
(ii) Costs incurred in purchasing the asset (estate agents' fees, legal fees, etc)

(c) **Enhancement expenditure**

This is capital expenditure which enhances the value of the asset and is reflected in the state or nature of the asset at the time of disposal.

Illustration 2: Calculation of capital gain

Jack bought a holiday cottage for £25,000. He paid legal costs of £600 on the purchase.

Jack spent £8,000 building an extension to the cottage.

Jack sold the cottage for £60,000. He paid estate agents' fees of £1,200 and legal costs of £750.

Jack's gain on sale is:

£	24,450

	£
Disposal consideration	60,000
Less incidental costs of disposal (1,200 + 750)	(1,950)
Net proceeds	58,050
Less allowable costs (25,000 + 600)	(25,600)
Less enhancement expenditure	(8,000)
Chargeable gain	24,450

Activity 1: Capital gain calculation

Mr Dunstable bought an asset for £12,700 in February 1986. He incurred legal fees of £500. He sold the asset for £38,500 incurring expenses of £1,500. While he owned the asset he improved it at a cost of £3,000.

Required

Complete the table showing Mr Dunstable's gain.

Solution

	£
Proceeds	
Less selling expenses	
Net proceeds	
Less cost	
Less legal fees on purchase	
Less enhancement	
Capital gain	

3 Computing taxable gains in a tax year

An individual pays capital gains tax (CGT) on any **taxable gains** arising in a **tax year** (6 April to 5 April).

All the chargeable gains made in the tax year are added together, and any capital losses made in the same tax year are deducted to give net gains (or losses) for the year. Next we deduct any unrelieved capital losses brought forward from previous years. Finally the annual exempt amount is deducted to arrive at taxable gains, on which CGT will be applied.

Illustration 3: Year-end computation

	£
Current gains	X
Current losses (all)	(X)
Net gains	X
Net capital gains	X
Annual exempt amount	(12,300)
Loss brought forward from earlier years	(X)
Taxable gains	X

Unused annual exempt amounts cannot be carried forward.

3.1 Annual exempt amount

Key term

Annual exempt amount This is the amount of capital gains a taxpayer may realise in a tax year before they have to pay capital gains tax.

For 2020/21 it is £12,300.

It is also known as the annual exemption.

All individuals are entitled to an annual exempt amount. This means that in 2020/21 an individual can make gains of up to £12,300 and they will be tax free. As you can see above, it is deducted from the total net gains for the year before the deduction of capital losses brought forward.

3.2 Losses

If losses have been made in the current year they must be offset against the gains of that year even if this means that some or all of the annual exempt amount is wasted.

If the losses in a year are greater than the gains then the excess losses are carried forward.

When a capital loss is carried forward it is set against net gains in the next tax year AFTER the deduction of the annual exempt amount. This means the taxpayer does not lose the benefit of the annual exempt amount.

Any further loss remaining is carried forward.

Illustration 4: Capital losses

(a) Tim has chargeable gains for 2020/21 of £25,000 and allowable losses of £16,000. As the losses are current year losses they must be fully relieved against the gains to produce net gains of £9,000, despite the fact that net gains are below the annual exempt amount.

Chargeable gains in tax year	25,000
Less losses in tax year	(16,000)
Net chargeable gains	9,000
Less annual exempt amount	(12,300)
Taxable gain	0

(b) Hattie has gains of £12,500 for 2020/21 and allowable losses brought forward of £6,000. Hattie restricts her loss relief to £200 so as to take the taxable gain down to nil.

	£
Net chargeable gains	12,500
Less annual exempt amount	(12,300)
Less capital loss brought forward	(200)
Taxable gain	0

The remaining £5,800 of losses will be carried forward to 2021/22.

Activity 2: Current year losses

In 2020/21, Ted makes gains of £45,000 and £10,000. He also makes a loss of £48,000. Ted has no losses to bring forward from earlier years.

Required

Complete the following sentences:

Ted's net capital gain for 2020/21 before the annual exempt amount

is £ [   ]

Ted has a loss to carry forward of £ [   ]

Activity 3: Prior year losses

Tara makes a gain on a property in 2020/21 of £12,800 (proceeds of £25,800 less cost of £13,000). She makes no other disposals in the tax year. Tara has losses brought forward from the previous year of £10,000.

Required

Complete the following sentences:

Tara's net capital gain for 2020/21 before the annual exempt amount

is £ [   ]

Tara has a loss to carry forward of £ [   ]

4 Computing capital gains tax (CGT) payable

An individual's taxable gains are chargeable to CGT at the rate of 10% or 20% depending on the individual's taxable income for 2020/21.

If the individual is a basic rate taxpayer, then CGT is payable at 10% on an amount of taxable gains up to the amount of the taxpayer's **unused** basic rate band and at 20% on the excess.

If the individual is a higher or additional rate taxpayer, then CGT is payable at 20% on all their taxable gains. Note the basic rate band covers taxable income and gains up to £37,500 (for 2020/21).

Note that a large gain may take a taxpayer out of the basic rate band and into the higher rate band. Don't forget that the bands will be extended by Gift Aid and/or personal pension scheme contributions.

Illustration 5: Calculating capital gains tax

(a) Sally has taxable income (ie the amount after the deduction of the personal allowance) of £10,000 in 2020/21 and made taxable gains (ie gains after deduction of the annual exempt amount) of £20,000 in 2020/21.

Sally's CGT liability is:

£20,000 × 10%   £2,000

The taxable income uses £10,000 of the basic rate band, leaving £27,500 of the basic rate band unused, therefore all of the taxable gain is taxed at 10%.

(b) Hector has taxable income of £50,000 in 2020/21 (ie he is a higher rate taxpayer). He made taxable gains of £10,000 in 2020/21.

Hector's CGT liability is:

£10,000 × 20%   £2,000

All of Hector's basic rate band has been taken up by the taxable income, therefore the taxable gain is taxed at 20%.

(c) Isabel has taxable income of £33,000 in 2020/21 and made taxable gains of £25,000 in 2020/21.

Isabel has (£37,500 – £33,000) = £4,500 of her basic rate band unused. Isabel's CGT liability is:

	£
4,500 × 10%	450
20,500 × 20%	4,100
25,000	4,550

Activity 4: Computing capital gains tax payable

Mr Dunstable (see Activity 1) had a chargeable gain of £20,800 in 2020/21. He has taxable income of £31,000.

Required

What is Mr Dunstable's capital gains tax payable?

£ [   ]

5 Self-assessment for CGT

5.1 Administration

CGT is payable on 31 January following the end of the tax year.

Unlike income tax there are no requirements for payments on account.

6 Special rules applying to specific disposals

Assessment focus point

The following rules need to be used in particular circumstances. Make sure you spot them in the assessment and apply them when required.

6.1 Part disposals and chattels

6.1.1 Part disposals

Sometimes part, rather than the whole, of an asset is disposed of. For instance, one-third of a piece of land may be sold. In this case, we need to be able to compute the chargeable gain or allowable loss arising on the part of the asset disposed of.

The problem is that, although we know what the disposal proceeds are for the part of the asset disposed of, we do not usually know what proportion of the 'cost' of the whole asset relates to that part. The solution to this is to **use the following fraction to determine the cost of the part disposed of**.

Formula to learn

The fraction is:

$$\frac{A}{A+B} = \frac{\text{Value of the part disposed of}}{\text{Value of the part disposed of} + \text{Market value of the remainder}}$$

A is the 'gross' proceeds (or market value) before deducting incidental costs of disposal.

B is the market value of the part of the asset that was not sold.

Illustration 6: Part disposal calculation

	£
Gross proceeds	X
Less selling costs	(X)
	X
Less:	
Original cost of the whole asset × $\dfrac{A}{A+B}$	(C)
Gain	X

Illustration 7: Part disposal

Mr Jones bought 4 acres of land for £270,000. He sold 1 acre of the land at auction for £200,000, before auction expenses of 15%. The market value of the 3 remaining acres is £460,000.

The cost of the land being sold is:

$$\frac{200,000}{200,000+460,000} \times £270,000 = £81,818$$

	£
Disposal proceeds	200,000
Less incidental costs of sale (15% × £200,000)	(30,000)
Net proceeds	170,000
Less cost (see above)	(81,818)
Chargeable gain	88,182

Activity 5: Part disposal

Tom bought 10 acres of land for £20,000.

He sold 3 acres of land for £10,000 incurring disposal costs of £950 when the remaining 7 acres were worth £36,000.

Required

Complete the following sentences:

The gain on the disposal of the land is   **£** [   ]

The cost of the remaining land carried forward is   **£** [   ]

6.1.2 Chattels

Chattels are tangible moveable property.

Wasting chattel is a chattel with an estimated remaining useful life of 50 years or less, eg a racehorse or greyhound.

Key term

Wasting chattels are exempt from CGT so there are no chargeable gains and no allowable losses.

Non-wasting chattels are chargeable to CGT in the normal way, subject to the following exceptions/restrictions.

Illustration 8: Rule for computing gains/losses on non-wasting chattels

Cost	Proceeds		
≤ 6,000	≤ 6,000	Wholly exempt	• No need to calculate any gain
≤ 6,000	> 6,000	Any gain restricted to max of: $^5/_3 \times$ (Gross proceeds – £6,000)	• Calculate gain, compare to the maximum, take the lower figure
> 6,000	≤ 6,000	Gross proceeds deemed to be £6,000	• Do normal calculation but always use £6,000 as gross proceeds figure
> 6,000	> 6,000	Wholly taxable	• Calculate a gain using the normal rules

Illustration 9: Proceeds > £6,000, Cost < £6,000

John purchased a painting for £3,000. On 1 January this year he sold the painting at auction.

If the gross sale proceeds are £4,000, the gain on sale will be exempt.

If the gross sale proceeds are £8,000 with costs of sale of 10%, the gain arising on the disposal of the painting will be calculated as follows:

	£
Gross proceeds	8,000
Less incidental costs of sale (10% × £8,000)	(800)
Net proceeds	7,200
Less cost	(3,000)
Chargeable gain	4,200
Gain cannot exceed $^5/_3 \times$ £(8,000 – 6,000)	3,333
Therefore chargeable gain is £3,333.	

Illustration 10: Proceeds < £6,000, Cost > £6,000

Magee purchased an antique desk for £8,000. She sold the desk in an auction for £4,750 net of auctioneer's fees of 5% in November.

Magee obviously has a loss and therefore the allowable loss is calculated on deemed proceeds of £6,000. The costs of disposal can be deducted from the deemed proceeds of £6,000.

	£
Deemed disposal proceeds	6,000
Less incidental costs of disposal (£4,750 × 5/95)	(250)
	5,750
Less cost	(8,000)
Allowable loss	(2,250)

Activity 6: Chattels

(a) Orlando Gibbons purchased a rare manuscript for £500. He sold it several years later for £9,000, before deducting the auctioneer's commission of £1,000.

(b) He also had an antique bought for £7,000 which he sold two years later for £3,000.

Required

Complete the following sentences:

(a) The chargeable gain on the disposal is £ [   ]

(b) The loss on the disposal is £ [   ]

6.2 Transfers to connected persons

If a disposal by an individual is made to a connected person, **the disposal is deemed to take place at the market value of the asset**.

If an **allowable loss arises** on the disposal, it can **only be set against gains** arising in the same or future tax years from disposals **to the same connected person**, and the loss can only be set off if they are still connected with the person making the loss.

For this purpose an individual is connected with:

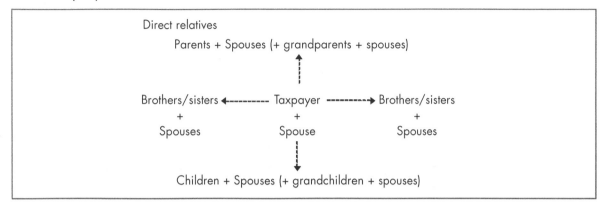

Direct relatives
Parents + Spouses (+ grandparents + spouses)

Brothers/sisters ◄-------- Taxpayer --------► Brothers/sisters
+   +   +
Spouses   Spouse   Spouses

Children + Spouses (+ grandchildren + spouses)

6.3 Transfers between spouses/civil partners

Spouses/civil partners are taxed as two separate people. Each individual has an annual exempt amount, and allowable losses of one individual cannot be set against gains of the other.

Disposals between spouses/civil partners do not give rise to chargeable gains or allowable losses. The disposal is said to be on a '**no gain/no loss**' basis. The acquiring spouse/civil partner takes the base cost of the disposing spouse/civil partner.

Activity 7: Transfers between spouses/civil partners

William sold an asset to his wife Kate in the current tax year for £32,000 when its market value was £45,000. William acquired the asset for £14,000 in June 2005.

Required

Calculate the chargeable gain on this transfer. Tick one box.

	✓
Nil	
£18,000	
£31,000	
£13,000	

7 Tax planning

Consider:

(a) Delaying sale of an asset until after the end of the tax year, this would give you a whole extra year until you had to pay the tax and allow you to use next year's annual exempt amount (if you have already used this year's).

(b) Spouses and civil partners may transfer assets at no gain no loss. This effectively transfers the asset over at its original cost so that the gain will be the same whichever party sells it. It therefore makes sense to ensure an asset is sold by the spouse/civil partner who:

- Pays tax at a lower rate
- Has an unused annual exemption
- Has capital losses

Chapter summary

- A chargeable gain arises when there is a chargeable disposal of a chargeable asset by a chargeable person.

- Enhancement expenditure can be deducted in computing a chargeable gain if it is reflected in the state and nature of the asset at the time of disposal.

- Taxable gains are net chargeable gains for a tax year (ie minus allowable losses of the current tax year and any unrelieved capital losses brought forward) minus the annual exempt amount.

- Losses brought forward are deducted AFTER deduction of the annual exempt amount.

- The rates of CGT are 10% and 20%, but the lower rate of 10% only applies if and to the extent that the individual has any unused basic rate band.

- CGT is payable by 31 January following the end of the tax year.

- On the part disposal of an asset the formula A/(A + B) must be applied to work out the cost attributable to the part disposed of.

- Wasting chattels are exempt assets (eg racehorses and greyhounds).

- If a non-wasting chattel is sold for gross proceeds of £6,000 or less and was bought for £6,000 or less then any gain arising is exempt.

- If gross proceeds exceed £6,000 on the sale of a non-wasting chattel but the cost is less than £6,000, any gain arising on the disposal of the asset is limited to 5/3 × (Gross proceeds − £6,000).

- If the gross proceeds are less than £6,000 on the sale of a non-wasting chattel but it was bought for more than £6,000 any loss otherwise arising is restricted by deeming the gross proceeds to be £6,000.

- A disposal to a connected person takes place at market value.

- For individuals, connected people are broadly brothers, sisters, lineal ancestors and descendants and their spouses/civil partners plus similar relations of a spouse/civil partner.

- Losses on disposals to connected people can only be set against gains on disposals to the same connected person.

- Disposals between spouses/civil partners take place on a no gain/no loss basis.

Keywords

- **Chargeable asset:** Any asset that is not an exempt asset
- **Chargeable disposal:** A sale or gift of an asset
- **Chargeable person:** An individual or company
- **Chattel:** Tangible moveable property
- **Connected person:** A close relation of the taxpayer or their spouse/civil partner
- **Enhancement expenditure:** Capital expenditure that enhances the value of the asset and is reflected in the state or nature of the asset at the time of disposal
- **Exempt disposal:** A disposal on which no chargeable gain or allowable loss arises
- **Part disposal:** When part of an, rather than a whole, asset is disposed of
- **Taxable gains:** The chargeable gains of an individual for a tax year, after deducting allowable losses of the same tax year, any unrelieved capital losses brought forward and the annual exempt amount
- **Wasting chattel:** A chattel with an estimated remaining useful life of 50 years or less

Test your learning

1   **Tick to show if the following disposals would be chargeable or exempt for CGT.**

	Chargeable ✓	Exempt ✓
A gift of an antique necklace		
The sale of a building		
Sale of a racehorse		

2   Janet bought a plot of land for £80,000. She spent £10,000 on drainage. She sold the land for £200,000.

   Using the proforma layout provided, compute the gain on sale.

	£
Proceeds of sale	
Less cost	
Less enhancement expenditure	
Chargeable gain	

3   Philip has chargeable gains of £171,000 and allowable losses of £5,300 in 2020/21. Losses brought forward at 6 April 2020 amount to £10,000.

   The amount liable to CGT in 2020/21 is:

   £ _____

   The losses carried forward are:

   £ _____

4   Martha is a higher rate taxpayer who made chargeable gains (before the annual exempt amount) of £24,800 in October 2020.

   Martha's CGT liability for 2020/21 is:

   £ _____

5   **The payment date for capital gains tax for 2020/21 is (insert date XX/XX/XXXX):**

   _____

123

6   Richard sells 4 acres of land (out of a plot of 10 acres) for £38,000 in July 2020. Costs of disposal amount to £3,000. The 10-acre plot cost £41,500. The market value of the 6 acres remaining is £48,000.

The chargeable gain/allowable loss arising is:

Tick ONE box.

	✓
£16,663	
£17,500	
£19,663	
£18,337	

7   Mustafa bought a non-wasting chattel for £3,500.

The gain arising if he sells it for:

(a) £5,800 after deducting selling expenses of £180 is:

£ [   ]

(b) £8,200 after deducting selling expenses of £220 is:

£ [   ]

8   **Decide whether the following statement is true or false.**

A loss arising on a disposal to a connected person can be set against any gains arising in the same tax year or in subsequent tax years.

	✓
True	
False	

9   **Decide whether the following statement is true or false.**

No gain or loss arises on a disposal to a spouse/civil partner.

	✓
True	
False	

10 **Complete the table by ticking the appropriate box for each scenario.**

	Actual proceeds used	Deemed proceeds (market value) used	No gain or loss basis
Paul sells an asset to his civil partner Joe for £3,600.			
Grandmother gives an asset to her grandchild worth £1,000.			
Sarah sells an asset worth £20,000 to her best friend Cathy for £12,000. Sarah knows the asset is worth £20,000.			

Share disposals

7

Learning outcomes

4	Account for capital gains tax
4.3	Calculate gains and losses arising on the disposal of shares
	• Apply matching rules for individuals
	• Account for bonus issues
	• Account for rights issues

Assessment context

Shares were tested for 10 marks in Task 10 of the initial AAT sample assessment. The task will be assessed by free data entry of all workings and will be human marked.

Qualification context

Share disposals by individuals also feature in *Business Tax*. You will not see these rules anywhere else in your qualification.

Business context

A tax practitioner needs to be able to calculate capital gains tax payable on the disposal of shares for their clients.

Chapter overview

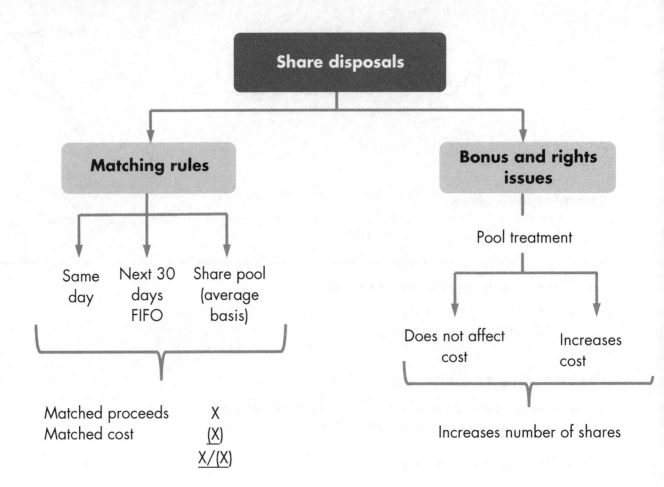

Introduction

In this chapter we are going to look at special rules that apply when shares are sold.

1 Share disposal rules

1.1 Matching rules

Shares present special problems when computing gains or losses on disposal. For instance, suppose that a taxpayer buys some shares in X plc on the following dates:

	No of shares	Cost £
5 July 1992	150	195
17 January 1997	100	375
2 July 2020	100	1,000

On 15 June 2020, he sells 220 of his shares for £3,300. **To work out his chargeable gain, we need to be able to identify which shares** out of his three holdings **were actually sold**. Since one share is identical to any other, it is not possible to work this out by reference to factual evidence.

As a result, it has been necessary to devise 'matching rules'. These allow us to identify on a disposal which shares have been sold and so **work out what the allowable cost** (and therefore the gain) **on disposal should be**. These matching rules are considered in detail below.

Assessment focus point

It is very important that you understand the matching rules. These rules are very regularly assessed and if you do not understand them you will not be able to get any part of the task right.

Formula to learn

Matching rules

Shares sold should be matched with purchases in the following order:

(1) Acquisitions on the same day as disposal.

(2) Acquisitions within the following 30 days on a first in, first out (FIFO) basis.

(3) Shares from the share pool. The share pool includes all other shares not acquired on the dates above, and is explained below.

Illustration 1: Matching rules

Noah acquired shares in Ark Ltd as follows.

2 August 2012   10,000 shares
25 April 2014   10,000 shares
17 June 2020   1,000 shares
19 June 2020   2,000 shares

Noah sold 15,000 shares on 17 June 2020.

Which shares is he selling for capital gains tax purposes?

Noah will match his disposal of 15,000 shares on 17 June 2020 as follows:

(1)   1,000 shares bought on 17 June 2020 (same day)
(2)   2,000 shares bought on 19 June 2020 (next 30 days, FIFO basis)
(3)   12,000 shares from the 20,000 shares in the share pool

Illustration 2: Basic computation

	£	£
For each batch of matched shares:		
Proportion of proceeds	X	
Less cost (if from share pool W1)	(X)	
		X

(W1) Share pool

	No of shares	Cost £
Shares bought/sold	X	X

1.2 Share pool

The share pool includes shares acquired up to the day before the disposal on which we are calculating the gain or loss. It grows when an acquisition is made and shrinks when a disposal is made.

1.2.1 The calculation of the share pool value

To compute the value of the share pool, set up two columns of figures:

(a)   The number of shares
(b)   The cost of the shares

Each time shares are acquired, both the number and the cost of the acquired shares are added to those already in the pool.

When there is a disposal from the pool, both the number of shares being disposed of and a cost relating to those shares are deducted from the pool. The cost of the disposal is calculated as a proportion of total cost in the pool, based on the number of shares being sold.

Illustration 3: The share pool

Jackie bought 10,000 shares in X plc for £6,000 in August 1996 and another 10,000 shares for £9,000 in December 2008.

She sold 12,000 shares for £24,000 in August 2020.

The gain is:

	£
Proceeds of sale	24,000
Less allowable cost (Workings)	(9,000)
Chargeable gain	15,000

Workings

The share pool is:

	No of shares	Cost £
August 1996 acquisition	10,000	6,000
December 2008 acquisition	10,000	9,000
	20,000	15,000
August 2020 disposal (£15,000 × 12,000/20,000 = £9,000)	(12,000)	(9,000)
c/f	8,000	6,000

Activity 1: Matching rules

Mr L made the following purchases of ordinary shares in H plc:

Date	Number	Cost
15 May 2002	2,200	8,800
1 May 2020	400	3,000
17 May 2020	500	4,500

On 1 May 2020 Mr L sold 1,600 shares for £14,000.

Required

What is the chargeable gain or loss for 2020/21 on the disposal of these shares? Clearly show the balance of shares to be carried forward.

Solution

	Number	£

Activity 2: Share pool

Mr Lambert purchased the following holdings in Grande plc:

Date	Number	Cost £
January 1985	3,000	5,000
February 1987	1,000	4,000

In May 2020 he sold 2,000 shares for £14,000.

Required

What is the chargeable gain or loss for 2020/21 on the disposal of these shares? Clearly show the balance of shares to be carried forward.

Solution

	Number	£

1.3 Bonus and rights issues

1.3.1 Bonus issues

Bonus issues are free shares given to existing shareholders in proportion to their existing shareholding. For example, a shareholder may own 2,000 shares. The company makes a 1 share for every 2 shares held bonus issue (called a 1 for 2 bonus issue). The shareholder will then have an extra 1,000 shares, giving them 3,000 shares overall.

Bonus shares are treated as being acquired at the date of the original acquisition of the underlying shares giving rise to the bonus issue.

Since bonus shares are issued at no cost there is **no need to adjust the original cost**.

1.3.2 Rights issues

In a **rights issue**, a **shareholder is offered the right to buy additional shares by the company in proportion to the shares already held**.

The difference between a bonus issue and a rights issue is that in a rights issue the new shares are paid for. This results in an **adjustment to the original cost**.

For matching purposes, bonus and rights shares are treated as if they were acquired on the same day as the shareholder's original holdings.

Illustration 4: Bonus and rights issues

Jonah acquired 20,000 shares for £34,200 in T plc in April 2005. There was a 1 for 2 bonus issue in May 2010 and a 1 for 5 rights issue in August 2015 at £1.20 per share.

Jonah sold 30,000 shares for £45,000 in December 2020.

The gain on sale is:

	£
Proceeds of sale	45,000
Less allowable cost (Workings)	(34,500)
Chargeable gain	10,500

Workings

The share pool is constructed as follows:

	No of shares	Cost £
April 2005 acquisition	20,000	34,200
May 2010 bonus 1 for 2 ($^1/_2$ × 20,000 = 10,000)	10,000	–
	30,000	34,200
August 2015 rights 1 for 5 @ £1.20 ($^1/_5$ × 30,000 = 6,000 shares × £1.20 = £7,200)	6,000	7,200
	36,000	41,400
December 2020 disposal (£41,400 × 30,000/36,000 = £34,500)	(30,000)	(34,500)
c/f	6,000	6,900

Activity 3: Bonus and rights issues

Richard had the following transactions in S plc.

1.10.95	Bought 10,000 shares for £15,000
11.9.99	Bought 2,000 shares for £5,000
1.2.00	Took up rights issue 1 for 2 at £2.75 per share
5.9.05	2 for 1 bonus issue
14.10.20	Sold 15,000 shares for £15,000

Required

Calculate the gain or loss made on these shares. All workings must be shown in your calculations.

Solution

	Number	£

2 Tax planning

The tax planning ideas we considered in the previous chapter are still relevant here. One further matter to consider is that a holding of shares can be easily split so if a married couple/civil partnership were going to sell some shares and realise a large gain they could split the ownership between them before the sale. Instead of realising one gain they now have one gain each meaning that they could both use their annual exempt amounts rather than leaving one to go to waste (assuming they had no other disposals in the year).

Chapter summary

- The matching rules are:
  - (1) Same day acquisitions
  - (2) Next 30 days' acquisitions on a FIFO basis
  - (3) Shares in the share pool
- The share pool runs up to the day before disposal.
- Bonus issue and rights issue shares are acquired in proportion to the shareholder's existing holding.

Keywords

- **Bonus shares:** Shares that are issued free to shareholders based on original holdings

- **Rights issues:** Similar to bonus issues except that in a rights issue shares must be paid for

Test your learning

1   Tasha bought 10,000 shares in V plc in August 1994 for £5,000 and a further 10,000 shares for £16,000 in April 2009. She sold 15,000 shares for £30,000 in November 2020.

   Tick to show what her chargeable gain is.

   Tick ONE box.

	✓
£15,750	
£11,500	
£17,000	
£14,250	

2   **Tick to show whether the following statement is true or false.**

   In both a bonus issue and a rights issue, there is an adjustment to the original cost of the shares.

	✓
True	
False	

3   Marcus bought 2,000 shares in X plc in May 2003 for £12,000. There was a 1 for 2 rights issue at £7.50 per share in December 2004. Marcus sold 2,500 shares for £20,000 in March 2021.

   His chargeable gain is:

   £ [   ]

4   Mildred bought 6,000 shares in George plc in June 2011 for £15,000. There was a 1 for 3 bonus issue in August 2012. Mildred sold 8,000 shares for £22,000 in December 2020.

   Her chargeable gain is:

   £ [   ]

5   **What are the share matching rules?**

Private residence relief

8

Learning outcomes

Having studied this chapter, you will be able to:

4	**Account for capital gains tax**
4.2	**Calculate chargeable gains and allowable losses** • Determine private residence relief

Assessment context

This topic is included in the syllabus but was not tested in the initial AAT sample assessment.

Qualification context

You will not be tested on these rules outside of this unit.

Business context

Selling a house could trigger a substantial capital gains tax liability. A practitioner needs to be able to recognise when these rules apply to reduce or exempt the gain.

Chapter overview

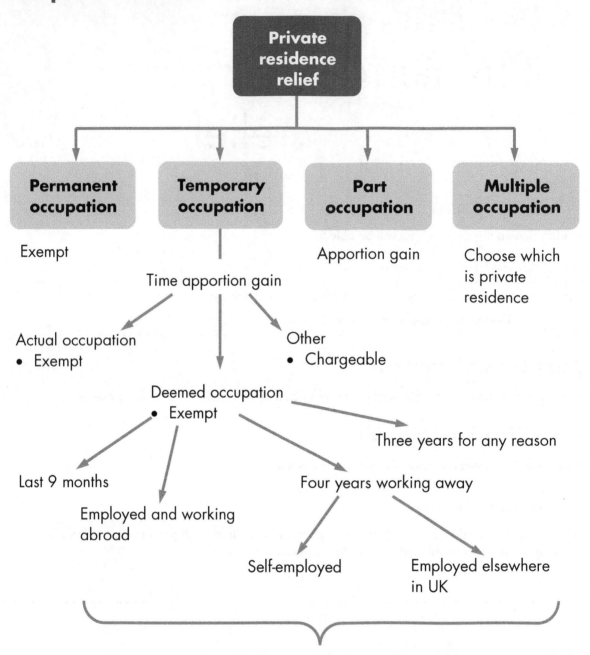

Private residence relief

Permanent occupation

Exempt

Temporary occupation

Time apportion gain

Part occupation

Apportion gain

Multiple occupation

Choose which is private residence

Actual occupation
- Exempt

Other
- Chargeable

Deemed occupation
- Exempt

Last 9 months

Employed and working abroad

Three years for any reason

Four years working away

Self-employed

Employed elsewhere in UK

Must have occupied before and after absence

Introduction

In this chapter we are going to look at special rules that apply when a taxpayer sells the property that they have lived in.

1 Private residence relief

1.1 General rule

Key term

Private residence This is an individual's only or main residence. It includes a garden of up to half a hectare. There is usually no capital gains tax liability when an individual sells their residence because of private residence relief.

If a taxpayer has lived in the residence **for the whole period of ownership** then there will be **no capital gain when the property is sold**. If the taxpayer has not lived there for the whole period of ownership than **only the gain relating to the period of occupation will be exempt**. This will be calculated by **time apportioning** the gain.

Likewise, if the property is sold at a loss then no capital loss may be claimed.

Formula to learn

Illustration – Private residence relief is calculated as:

$$\text{Gain} \times \frac{\text{Period of occupation}}{\text{Period of ownership}}$$

1.2 Periods of occupation

Even though the taxpayer may not actually be occupying the property we may be able to treat it for tax purposes as if the taxpayer was actually in residence thus giving exemption from tax. These are what we call periods of **deemed occupation**.

Key term

Deemed occupation A period of time when HMRC will treat the taxpayer as occupying the property for the purposes of claiming private residence relief even though they are not actually there.

The last nine months are always deemed occupation in full, provided the property was the taxpayer's private residence at some point.

Certain periods of absence are deemed occupation, providing that they are preceded and followed (at any time whatsoever) by actual occupation:

Deemed occupation

- Any period during which the owner was abroad by reason of their employment

- Any periods (not exceeding four years in total) during which the employed owner was required to work away from home in the UK

- Any periods (not exceeding four years in total) during which the owner, if self-employed, was working away from home in the UK or overseas

- Any periods, for whatever reason, not exceeding three years in total. Where a period of absence exceeds three years, three years out of the longer period are deemed to be a period of occupation.

1.3 Part occupation

If any part of the residence is not occupied by the owner for residence purposes, private residence relief will be proportionately withdrawn. For example, if the garage was used as a workshop and one bedroom was used as a home office for a business, then the private residence would only be available on the percentage used for residential purposes.

If the property had been used for different purposes at different times then there would need to be an apportionment of relief based on time and use.

1.4 More than one residence

The taxpayer may choose which home is to be their private residence, provided that each has been occupied at some point.

If the owner is unable to occupy their own home because they are required to occupy job-related accommodation, their own home will be deemed to be their main residence, provided that they intend to occupy it at some point.

1.5 More than one occupier

Married couples/civil partners are only allowed one exemption between them.

Illustration 1: Private residence relief

Mr A purchased a house for £50,000 on 31 March 2001. He lived in the house until 30 June 2001. He was then sent to work abroad by his employer for five years before returning to the UK to live in the house again on 1 July 2006. He stayed in the house for fifteen months before moving out to live with friends until the house was sold on 31 December 2020 for £150,000.

First work out the total period of ownership:

31 March 2001 to 31 December 2020 = 19 years and 9 months (or 237 months).

Next, decide what periods are chargeable and which are exempt:

		Exempt months	Chargeable months
(i)	31 March 2001 to 30 June 2001	3	–
(ii)	1 July 2001 to 30 June 2006	60	–
(iii)	1 July 2006 to 30 September 2007	15	–
(iv)	1 October 2007 to 31 March 2020	–	150
(v)	1 April 2020 to 31 December 2020	9	–
		87	150

Explanations:

(i)   **April 2001 to June 2001.** Actual occupation.

(ii) **July 2001 to June 2006.** Covered by the exemption for periods of absence during which the owner is required by his employment to live abroad. The period is both preceded and followed by a period of owner occupation.

(iii) **July 2006 to September 2007.** Actual occupation.

(iv) **October 2007 to March 2020.** This period is not eligible to be partly covered by the exemption for three years of absence for any reason, as it is not followed by a period of actual occupation.

(v)   **April 2020 to December 2020.** Covered by the final nine months' exemption.

Then, calculate the chargeable gain after the exemption has been applied:

	£
Disposal proceeds	150,000
Less cost	(50,000)
Gain before private residence relief	100,000
Less exempt under private residence relief provisions	
87/237 × £100,000	(36,709)
Chargeable gain	63,291

In this example, had Mr A gone straight to live with friends in July 2006 instead of having six months' occupation, he would have lost not only the extra six months but also the period from July 2001 to June 2006. This period of absence would lose its status of deemed occupation as the property would not have been occupied again by the owner prior to sale.

Activity 1: Private residence relief

Harry bought his house in London on 1 April 1994 and lived in it until 1 April 1995. From that date until 1 April 1997, he was required by his employers to work overseas.

He returned to the UK on 1 April 1997 to work for his employers in Bristol but lived in rented accommodation there as it was too far to travel daily from London to Bristol to work. He returned to the house on 1 April 2000 for 15 months. From then on, he moved out to go and live with his mother where he remained until he sold his house on 30 September 2020, realising a gain of £100,000.

Required

Complete the following sentence:

The gain on the disposal of his house is £ ⬚ .

2 Tax planning

For most of the periods of deemed residence a taxpayer has to occupy the property before and after the period of absence. It is vital therefore that the taxpayer returns to the property after a period of absence to ensure they get the exemption. Also, if a taxpayer moves away and plans to sell the house they should try to do it within the nine month window to prevent a gain accruing.

Chapter summary

- Any gain arising on the disposal of an individual's private residence is exempt from CGT if the individual has occupied/deemed to have occupied the property throughout the period of ownership. A loss on disposal is not allowable.

- If there have been periods of non-occupation, then part of any gain on disposal may be chargeable.

- Certain periods of non-occupation count as periods of deemed occupation.

- The last nine months of ownership always count as a period of occupation if, at some time, the residence has been the taxpayer's main residence.

Keywords

- **Deemed occupation:** Periods during which an individual is treated as having occupied a residence

- **Private residence:** An individual's only or main residence

Test your learning

1 Provided the property has at some time been the owner's private residence, the last
.... months of ownership is always an exempt period.

Tick ONE box.

	✓
6	
9	
18	
24	

2 **Explain three examples of periods of absence from a property which are deemed periods of occupation for the CGT private residence exemption.**

3 Josephine purchased a house on 1 April 2003 for £60,000 and used it as her main residence until 1 August 2006 when she was sent by her employer to manage the Paris office. She worked and lived in Paris until 31 July 2010. Josephine returned to live in the house on 1 August 2010 but moved out to live in a new house (to be treated as her main residence) on 1 February 2013. The property was empty until sold on 30 November 2020 for £180,000.

Using the proforma below, compute the gain on sale.

	£
Proceeds	
Cost	
Gain before private residence exemption	
Private residence exemption	
Chargeable gain	

4   Noddy is selling his main residence, which he has owned for 25 years. He lived in the house for the first 14 years of ownership then, for the next 5 years, he was posted abroad by his employer. He never returned to live in the house during the remainder of his period of ownership.

What fraction of his gain will be exempt under the private residence exemption?

Tick ONE box.

	✓
19.75/25	
14/25	
14.75/25	
19/25	

5   Clare bought herself a flat in April 2014 for £80,000. She lived in the flat until October 2020 when she moved to a farmhouse she had bought to be her main residence. The flat was empty until it was sold in March 2021 for £300,000.

Decide whether the following statement is true or false.

Tick ONE box.

The gain arising on the sale is completely exempt.

	✓
True	
False	

Inheritance tax

9

Learning outcomes

1	Analyse the theories, principles and rules that underpin taxation systems
1.4	**Discuss residence and domicile** • The definitions of residence and domicile • The impact that each of these has on the taxation position of a UK taxpayer
5	**Discuss the basics of inheritance tax**
5.1	**Identify the basic features of chargeable lifetime and exempt transfers** • Chargeable lifetime transfers • Exempt transfers • Potential exempt transfers • Small gifts £250, gifts re marriage or civil partnership, normal expenditure out of income, annual transfers £3,000, transfers between spouses etc., gifts to charities, gifts to political parties and tapering relief • The basics of a transfer into trust
5.2	**Perform basic inheritance tax computations** • Calculate tax payable on death • Calculate tax payable on lifetime transfers • Identify who is responsible for payment of inheritance tax

Assessment context

Inheritance tax is worth 12% of the total syllabus so in your assessment you should expect to see questions worth approximately 12% of the total marks available.

In the initial sample assessment released by the AAT, Task 12 tested various inheritance tax rules for 6 marks while Task 13 required you to input a detailed inheritance tax calculation into a free text box for 6 marks.

Qualification context

You will not see the information in this chapter outside of this unit.

Business context

A tax practitioner may have to advise a taxpayer how to structure their tax affairs during lifetime to minimise the tax liability on their death. A practitioner may have to perform lifetime inheritance tax calculations for their clients and produce inheritance tax calculations on behalf of the executors of clients who have died.

Chapter overview

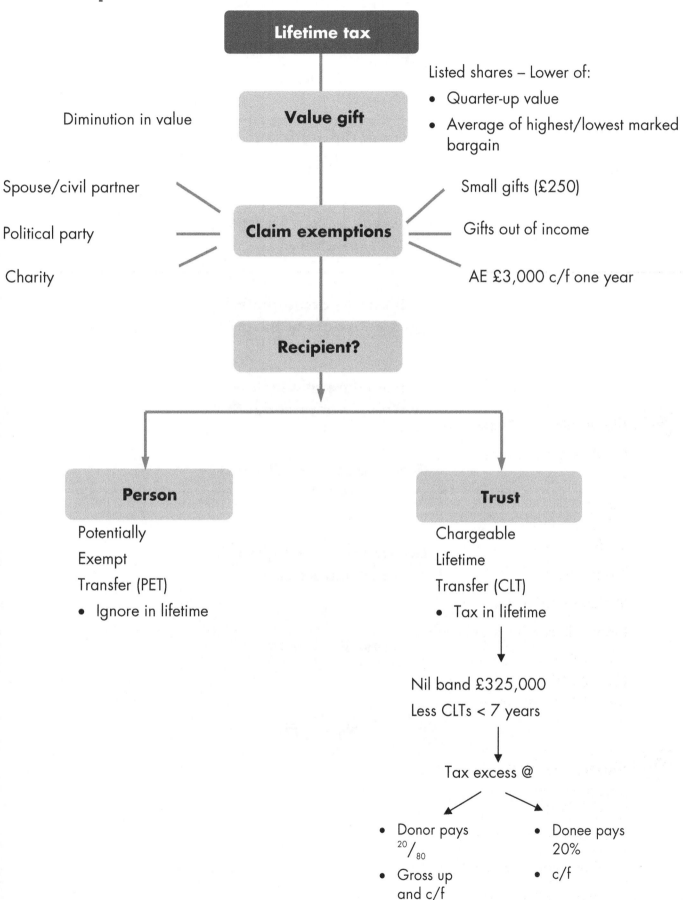

Lifetime tax

Listed shares – Lower of:
- Quarter-up value
- Average of highest/lowest marked bargain

Diminution in value

Value gift

Spouse/civil partner

Political party

Charity

Claim exemptions

Small gifts (£250)

Gifts out of income

AE £3,000 c/f one year

Recipient?

Person

Potentially
Exempt
Transfer (PET)
- Ignore in lifetime

Trust

Chargeable
Lifetime
Transfer (CLT)
- Tax in lifetime

Nil band £325,000
Less CLTs < 7 years

Tax excess @

- Donor pays $^{20}/_{80}$
- Gross up and c/f

- Donee pays 20%
- c/f

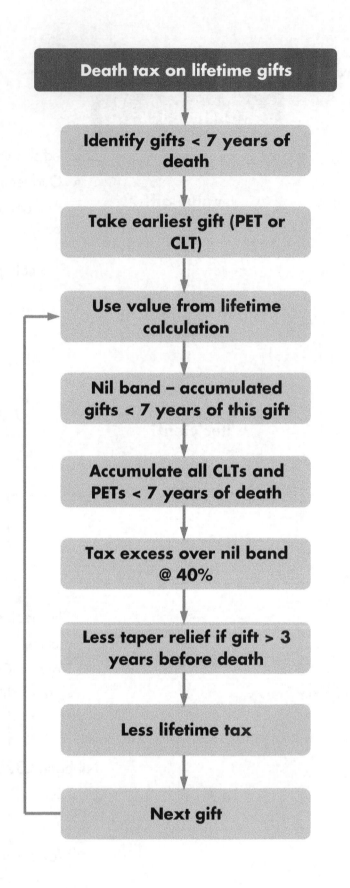

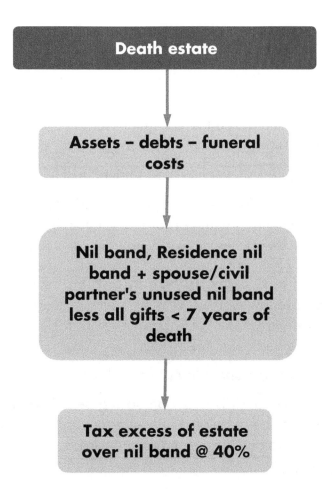

Introduction

Key term

Inheritance tax This is a tax on the transfer of wealth. Inheritance tax is sometimes abbreviated to IHT.

Only individuals pay inheritance tax. It is not levied on companies or partnerships.

Don't make the mistake of thinking inheritance tax is only applicable on death, it can also apply to transfers of wealth made during lifetime.

Transfer of wealth This is when a taxpayer deliberately gives away their wealth and receives either nothing in return or fails to obtain full value from the recipient. Inheritance tax therefore catches gifts or deliberate sales at undervalue.

Note that there has to be a **gratuitous intent**, meaning that the taxpayer must have intended to give away their wealth. There is therefore no inheritance tax charge if a tax payer simply makes a bad bargain, for example selling a painting for £500 that turns out to be worth £5,000.

Questions will therefore talk about 'transfers' or 'gifts'.

To calculate inheritance tax it is important to realise it is a three-stage process. All the three stages have to be calculated in the correct order as the first stage will have an impact on the second and the second on the third.

The three stages are:

- Lifetime tax paid on lifetime transfers
- Death tax paid on lifetime transfers made in the seven years prior to death
- Death tax paid on assets owned at death (death estate)

1 Residence and domicile issues

Domicile is the key issue for inheritance tax. We will cover the definition of domicile in more detail in Chapter 10, however for now it is enough to understand that a person's country of domicile is the country they consider to be home.

If a taxpayer is UK domiciled they will be chargeable to inheritance tax on all the assets they own regardless of the location of the assets.

If a taxpayer is not UK domiciled they will be only taxed on assets located within the UK.

We will now consider the three stages in the computation. The first is the lifetime tax paid on lifetime transfers.

2 Lifetime tax paid on lifetime transfers

This is when a taxpayer makes a gift during lifetime which is subject to inheritance tax.

Key term

Donor The person giving a gift.

Donee The person receiving the gift.

Tax is calculated with reference to the tax year.

The first step is always to value the gift.

2.1 Value of the transfer

The value of the transfer is calculated using the **diminution in value** principle.

In many cases the diminution in value of the donor's estate will be the same as the increase in the value of the donee's estate, for example if there is a cash gift or the gift of a house. However, sometimes the two will not be the same. Typically this is the situation where unquoted shares are gifted.

The measure of the transfer for inheritance tax purposes is always the loss to the donor (the diminution in value of their estate), not the amount gained by the donee.

Illustration 1: Diminution in value

Audrey wishes to give 200 shares to her son, Brian. The shares are only worth £2.50 each to Brian, since Brian will have only a small minority holding in the company. However, they were worth £15 each to Audrey as they gave her control of the company. After the gift Audrey will hold 4,900 shares and the value of these shares will be £10 each. The value per share to Audrey falls from £15 to £10 per share since she will lose control of the company.

The diminution in value of Audrey's estate is £27,500, as follows.

	£
Before the gift: 5,100 shares × £15	76,500
After the gift: 4,900 shares × £10	(49,000)
Diminution in value	27,500

Activity 1: Diminution of value

Mr Jones owns 75% of Hill Jones Ltd, an unquoted investment company. He gives a 30% holding to his son.

Shareholdings on this date were valued at:

Shareholding	£
75%	370,000
45%	200,000
30%	105,000

Required

What is the value of the gift for inheritance tax purposes?

£ [   ]

2.2 Listed shares

Note there are special rules that apply when the gift is of listed shares.

Quoted shares and securities are valued at the lower of:

- The 'quarter-up' value: lower quoted price plus ¼ (higher quoted price – lower quoted price)

- The average of the highest and lowest marked bargains

> **Illustration 2: Valuing listed shares**
>
> Shares in A plc are given away. On the day of the disposal they are quoted at 100–110p. The highest and lowest marked bargains were 99p and 110p.
>
> The value per share is the lower of:
>
> (a) $100 + ¼ (110 - 100) = 102.5p$
> (b) $(110 + 99) / 2 = 104.5p$
>
> The value per share is 102.5p.

2.3 Exemptions

Once we have valued the gift we then need to consider whether it is eligible for exemptions.

Some exemptions are only available on lifetime gifts while others are available on both lifetime and death gifts.

There are far more exemptions available during lifetime than on death so from a tax planning perspective it usually makes sense to give assets away during lifetime and use the exemptions to reduce the tax bill rather than allowing them to pass on your death when it is likely that more tax will have to be paid.

2.3.1 Exemptions that are always available during lifetime and on death

2.3.1.1 Transfers between spouses/civil partners

Any transfers of value between spouses/civil partners are exempt. The exemption covers lifetime gifts between them and property passing under a will or on intestacy. Intestacy is when the taxpayer has not made a will so their assets pass on to relatives following rules created by the Government.

2.3.1.2 Transfers to charities/political parties

These are always exempt.

2.3.2 Exemptions only available during lifetime

2.3.2.1 The small gifts exemptions

Outright gifts to individuals totalling £250 or less per donee in any one tax year are exempt. If gifts total more than £250 the whole amount is chargeable. A donor can give up to £250 each year to each of as many donees as they wish. The small gifts exemption cannot apply to gifts into trusts. We will discuss trusts later.

2.3.2.2 The annual exemption (AE)

The first £3,000 of value transferred in a tax year is exempt from IHT. The **annual exemption** is used only after all other exemptions (such as for transfers to spouses/civil partners). If several gifts are made in a year, the £3,000 exemption is applied to earlier gifts before later gifts.

Any unused portion of the annual exemption is carried forward for one year only. Only use it the following year after that year's annual exemption has been used.

Illustration 3: Annual exempt amount

Frank has no unused annual exemption brought forward at 6 April 2019.

On 1 August 2019 he makes a transfer of £600 to his son Peter.

On 1 September 2019 he makes a transfer of £2,000 to his nephew Quentin.

On 1 July 2020 he makes a transfer of £3,300 to a trust for his grandchildren.

On 1 June 2021 he makes a transfer of £5,000 to his friend Rowan.

Show the application of the annual exemptions.

2019/20	£
1.8.19 Gift to Peter	600
Less AE 2019/20	(600)
	0

	£
1.9.19 Gift to Quentin	2,000
Less AE 2019/20	(2,000)
	0

The unused annual exemption carried forward is £3,000 – £600 – £2,000 = £400.

2020/21	£	£
1.7.20 Gift to trust		3,300
Less: AE 2020/21	3,000	
AE 2019/20 b/f	300	
		(3,300)
		0

The unused annual exemption carried forward is zero because the 2020/21 exemption must be used before the 2019/20 exemption brought forward. The balance of £100 of the 2019/20 exemption is lost, because it cannot be carried forward for more than one year.

2021/22	£
1.6.21 Gift to Rowan	5,000
Less AE 2021/22	(3,000)
	2,000

2.3.2.3 Normal expenditure out of income

Inheritance tax is a tax on transfers of capital, not income. A transfer of value is exempt if:

(a)   It is made as part of the normal expenditure of the donor

(b)   Taking one year with another, it was made out of income

(c)   It leaves the donor with sufficient income to maintain their usual standard of living

As well as covering such things as regular presents this exemption can cover regular payments out of income such as a grandchild's school fees or the payment of life assurance premiums on a policy for someone else.

2.3.2.4 Gifts in consideration of marriage/civil partnership

Gifts in consideration of marriage/civil partnership are exempt up to:

(a)   £5,000 if from a parent of a party to the marriage/civil partnership

(b)   £2,500 if from a remoter ancestor or from one of the parties to the marriage/civil partnership

(c)   £1,000 if from any other person

The limits apply to gifts from any one donor for any one marriage/civil partnership. The exemption is available only if the marriage/civil partnership actually takes place. This exemption is deducted before the annual exemption.

Assessment focus point

These exemptions are given to you in the assessment.

Illustration 4: Exemptions

Dale made a gift of £153,000 to her son on 17 October 2015 on the son's marriage. Dale gave £100,000 to her spouse on 1 January 2020. Dale gave £70,000 to her daughter on 11 May 2020. The only other gifts Dale made were birthday and Christmas presents of £100 each to her grandchildren.

The following exemptions are available in respect of these transfers:

17 October 2015

	£
Gift to Dale's son	153,000
Less: ME	(5,000)
AE 2015/16	(3,000)
AE 2014/15 b/f	(3,000)
	142,000

1 January 2020

	£
Gift to Dale's spouse	100,000
Less spouse exemption	(100,000)
	0

11 May 2020

	£
Gift to Dale's daughter	70,000
Less: AE 2020/21	(3,000)
AE 2019/20 b/f	(3,000)
	64,000

The gifts to the grandchildren are covered by the small gifts exemption.

2.4 Is the gift taxable during lifetime?

Once we have valued the gift and deducted any exemptions we now need to consider whether it is actually taxable during lifetime.

A lifetime gift can be one of two things:

Key term

Potentially Exempt Transfer (PET) This is a gift to an individual. It is not taxable during lifetime but will be charged to inheritance tax if the donor dies within seven years of making the gift.

Chargeable Lifetime Transfer (CLT) This is a gift to a trust. It is immediately chargeable to inheritance tax during lifetime and will be charged to tax a second time if the donor dies within seven years of making the gift.

A trust arises when the law recognises that one party (the trustee(s)) is/are looking after an asset on behalf of another person/people (the beneficiary/beneficiaries).

Note that although PETs are not chargeable during lifetime it is important to consider them as they will use annual exemptions that could have been used by CLTs and if the taxpayer dies within seven years of making the PET, we will have to tax them.

There is an important tax planning point here. When CLTs and PETs are made in the same year the CLTs should be made first to use any available annual exemptions. If used up against the PETs the exemption(s) will be wasted if the donor survives seven years as the PET then will never be chargeable.

2.5 Calculation of lifetime tax on CLTs

Lifetime inheritance tax on lifetime transfers is chargeable at two rates of tax: a 0% rate (the 'nil rate') and 20%. The nil rate is chargeable where **accumulated transfers** do not exceed the **nil rate band** limit. The excess is chargeable at 20%.

The nil rate band is £325,000.

> **Accumulated transfers** These are CLTs made in the previous seven years.

2.5.1 Donee pays the tax

When a CLT is made and the donee (ie the trustee) pays the lifetime tax, follow these steps to work out the lifetime inheritance tax on it:

Step 1

Compute the value of the CLT. You may be given this in the question or you may have to work out the diminution of value or use the listed shares rules. You would then deduct exemptions (such as the annual exemption).

Step 2

Look back seven years from the date of the transfer to see if any other CLTs have been made. If so, these transfers use up the nil rate band available for the current transfer. This is called seven-year accumulation. Work out the value of any nil rate band still available.

Step 3

Any part of the CLT covered by the nil rate band is taxed at 0%. Any part of the CLT not covered by the nil rate band is charged at 20%.

Illustration 5: Tax payable by trustees

Eric makes a gift of £336,000 to a trust on 10 July 2020. The trustees agree to pay the tax due.

Calculate the lifetime tax payable by the trustees if Eric has made a lifetime chargeable transfer of value of £100,000 in August 2013.

Step 1

Value of CLT after exemptions (2 × £3,000) is £330,000.

Step 2

Lifetime transfer of value of £100,000 in seven years before 10 July 2020 (transfers after 10 July 2013). Nil rate band of £(325,000 – 100,000) = £225,000 is available.

Step 3

	IHT £
£225,000 × 0%	0
£105,000 × 20%	21,000
£330,000	21,000

IHT due of £21,000

2.5.2 Donor pays the tax

Consider the situation where the donor has already made gifts over the nil rate band of £325,000. Any further gifts made will be subject to inheritance tax at 20%.

Imagine the donor wants the trust to have an additional £100,000. If the donor gives the trust £100,000 the trustee will have to account for tax at 20%. The trustee pays £20,000 leaving £80,000 in the trust. The trust now does not have the full amount the donor wanted it to have!

To get round this problem the donor may give the trust the amount they wanted the trust to have and then pay an additional sum to cover the tax payable on this amount. This is known as **grossing up** the gift.

The gross amount (gift + tax) represents 100%, the tax 20% and the amount after tax has been paid (**the net**) represents 80%. So if the donor wants the trust to have £100,000 and this represents 80%, the tax payable would be £100,000 × $^{20}/_{80}$ = £25,000 and the gross amount £125,000 (£100,000 + £25,000). We can check this. If the donor pays £125,000 the tax is 20% of this, £25,000 leaving £100,000 for the trust.

It is normally assumed that the donor will pay the tax so the applicable rate is $^{20}/_{80}$ which can be simplified to 25% or $^{1}/_{4}$.

Assessment focus point

Read the question carefully to identify who is paying the tax. If the question is silent assume it is the donor who is paying the tax and use the $^{20}/_{80}$ rate.

Note that a gift made now will impact on later gifts and may be taxed again if the donor dies within seven years of making the gift. It is important to therefore identify the value of the gift carried forward. If the donor pays the tax the loss to the donor is not the net gift but the gross amount as they have paid tax on top of the amount received by the trust. It is therefore the gross amount that is carried forward.

If the donor is paying the tax then our steps are slightly different.

Step 1

Compute the value of the gift. You may be given this in the question or you may have to work it out.

Step 2

Look back seven years from the date of the transfer to see if any other CLTs have been made. If so, these transfers use up the nil rate band available for the current transfer. Work out the value of any nil rate band still available.

Step 3

Any part of the CLT covered by the nil rate band is taxed at 0%. Any part of the CLT not covered by the nil rate band is taxed at $^{20}/_{80}$.

Step 4

Work out the gross transfer by adding the net transfer and the tax together. You can check your figure by working out the tax on the gross transfer.

Illustration 6: Tax payable by donor

James makes a gift of £336,000 to a trust on 10 July 2020. James will pay the tax due.

Calculate the lifetime tax payable, if James has made a lifetime chargeable transfer of value of £100,000 in August 2013.

Step 1

Value of gift after exemptions (2 × £3,000) is £330,000.

Step 2

Lifetime transfer of value of £100,000 in seven years before 10 July 2020 (transfers after 10 July 2013). Nil rate band of £(325,000 − 100,000) = £225,000 available.

Step 3

	IHT £
£225,000 × 0%	0
£105,000 × $^{20}/_{80}$	26,250
£330,000	26,250

Step 4

Gross transfer is £(330,000 + 26,250) = £356,250.

Check: Tax on the gross transfer would be:

	IHT £
£225,000 × 0%	0
£131,250 × 20%	26,250
£356,250	26,250

2.6 Lifetime tax summary

- Value gift
    - Diminution in value
- Deduct reliefs and exemptions
    - Marriage exemption
    - A/E(s)
    - Small gifts
- Is the gift a CLT or PET?
    - PET – ignore in lifetime
    - CLT – tax it!
- Deduct available nil band – £325,000 less any CLTs in the previous seven years
- Tax excess at 25% ($^{20}/_{80}$) if donor pays or 20% if trust pays (if question is silent assume donor pays it)
- Gross value of gift (gross chargeable transfers (GCT))
    - = Gift (after all reliefs and exemptions) plus tax if donor pays
    - = Just gift (after all reliefs and exemptions) if trust pays

Illustration 7: Lifetime tax proforma

		£
Lifetime tax:		
Gift		X
Less AE		(X)
Less AE b/f		(X)
Net gift after exemptions		X
Less nil band remaining:		
Nil band at date of gift	X	
Less GCTs in last 7 years before gift	(X)	
		(X)
		X
Tax @ 20% (or $^{20}/_{80}$)		X

The gross chargeable transfer (GCT) which will use up the nil band for future gifts is calculated as follows:

		£
Net gift after exemptions		X
Tax paid by donor at $^{20}/_{80}$		X
		GCT

Activity 2: Calculating lifetime tax – CLTs only

Mr Butcher put £337,000 into a trust on 13 August 2020 having already put £116,000 into a trust three years earlier (the gross chargeable transfer was £110,000 after annual exemptions).

Required

Calculate the IHT payable when the trust is set up on 13 August 2020 and the gross chargeable transfer carried forward assuming:

(a) The trust agrees to pay the tax

The tax payable is   £ [   ]

The gross chargeable transfer is   £ [   ]

(b) Mr Butcher pays the tax

The tax payable is £ [   ]

The gross chargeable transfer is £ [   ]

Activity 3: Calculating lifetime tax – PETs and CLTs

Mr Beale put £343,000 into a trust on 13 August 2020 (trustees agreeing to pay the tax) having given £50,000 to his daughter on 15 March 2020. He gave £30,000 to his son on 19 August 2020.

Required

Calculate how much inheritance tax is payable on the:

(a) Gift to daughter

The tax is £ [   ]

(b) Gift to trust

The tax is £ [   ]

(c) Gift to son

The tax is £ [   ]

---

3 Death tax paid on lifetime transfers made in the seven years prior to death

Having considered the inheritance tax paid during lifetime the next step is to calculate inheritance tax payable on gifts made in the seven years prior to death.

Inheritance tax is charged on both PETs and CLTs made in the seven years prior to death.

It is important to note that gifts made more than seven years prior to the date of death will escape being charged to death tax. If the gift was a PET it would not have been taxed in lifetime either so we can now say it is no longer **potentially** exempt, it **is** exempt.

Note. also that if a taxpayer survives more than three years after making the gift then the tax payable will be reduced by **taper relief**.

It is therefore an important tax planning point that wealth should be given away as soon as possible. If the donor survives seven years after making the gift there will be no death tax. If the donor survives at least three years there will be death tax but this will be reduced by taper relief. The longer the taxpayer waits before making the gift the less likely it is they will survive long enough to escape/reduce death tax.

Note. that the death tax is always paid by the recipient of the gift.

Follow these steps to work out the death tax on the lifetime gifts.

Step 1

Identify the date of death. Look back seven years and identify all lifetime transfers made in this period. These are now **chargeable** regardless as to whether they were made to a person or a trust.

Step 2

Start with the earliest gift made in the seven years prior to death:

(a) Establish the gross chargeable amount (this would have been done for CLTs in the lifetime calculation above ie value it, deduct exemptions, gross up for lifetime tax if necessary).

(b) Take the nil rate band at death and look back seven years from the date of the gift to see if there are any earlier gifts that will reduce the amount of nil rate band. Note that CLTs made more than seven years prior to the date of death will reduce the available nil rate band but PETs made more than seven years prior to death are now exempt so can be ignored.

(c) Deduct the remaining nil band from the gift under consideration and tax any excess at the **death rate** of 40%.

(d) Taper the tax if the gift was made more than three years before the date of death.

(e) Deduct any lifetime tax paid. The death tax can be reduced to nil but a tax refund cannot be generated.

Step 3

Repeat Step 2 for the next gift made in the seven-year period prior to death. Note that when considering whether any of the nil band remains CLTs will always reduce the nil band regardless of when they were made but PETs will only reduce the nil band if made within seven years prior to the date of death.

Step 4

Repeat Step 2 for the next gift. Repeat for each of the gifts made in the seven years prior to death.

The taper relief rates are as follows:

Years before death	% reduction
Over three but less than four years	20
Over four but less than five years	40
Over five but less than six years	60
Over six but less than seven years	80

Illustration 8: Death tax on lifetime gifts

Boris Kartovski dies on 15 September 2020. You establish he has made the following gifts during his lifetime:

24 July 2009 CLT – gross chargeable transfer £300,000, no life time tax

1 August 2013 – PET – value after exemptions £500,000

13 January 2015 PET – value after exemptions £100,000

23 July 2017 CLT – gross chargeable transfer £400,000, life time tax £15,000

(At the date of this gift during lifetime the full nil band would have been available as the only gifts in the previous seven years were PETs. The donee paid the tax – (£400,000 – £325,000) × 20% = £15,000. As the donee paid the3 tax there is no need to gross up the gift.)

Refer to the following diagram as we work through the illustration.

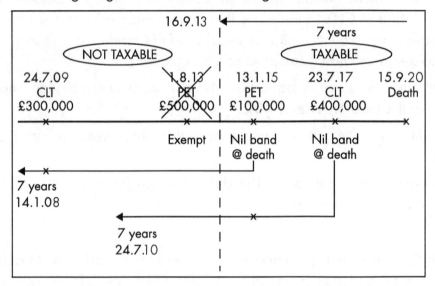

Step 1

Boris dies on 15 September 2020. All gifts made in the previous seven years are taxable regardless as to whether they were CLTs or PETs during lifetime. We are therefore interested in gifts made in the period 16 September 2013 to 15 September 2020.

Step 2

The earliest gift made in the seven years prior to death is the PET made on 13 January 2015. This is now chargeable to death tax.

(a) The gross chargeable amount is £100,000.

(b) The nil rate band at death is £325,000. If we look back seven years from 13 January 2015 to 14 January 2008 we see two earlier gifts made on the 24 July 2009 and 1 August 2013. One of these is a PET made more than seven years prior to the date of death so we can ignore it. The other though is a CLT so it will reduce our nil band. The nil band is therefore £325,000 – £300,000 = £25,000.

(c) The death tax on the gift is therefore (£100,000 – £25,000) × 40% = £30,000.

(d) The gift was made on 13 January 2015 and death occurred on 15 September 2020 so Boris survived five years after the date of the gift but not six years. Taper relief is therefore 60% so 40% of the tax is chargeable £30,000 × 40% = £12,000.

(e) This was a PET so there is no lifetime tax to deduct. The tax due is therefore £12,000.

Step 3

The next gift is the CLT made on 23 July 2017. This is now chargeable to death tax.

(a) The gross chargeable amount is £400,000.

(b) The nil rate band is £325,000. If we look back seven years to 24 July 2010 we see two earlier gifts made on 1 August 2013 and 13 January 2015. Both were PETs in lifetime. The earlier PET was made more than seven years prior to the date of death so can be ignored. The later PET though has become chargeable to death tax so must be included in our calculation. The nil rate band is therefore £325,000 – £100,000 = £225,000. Note that the earlier CLT of £300,000 made on 24 July 2009 is now out of range.

(c) The death tax on the gift is therefore (£400,000 – £225,000) × 40% = £70,000.

(d) The gift was made on 23 July 2017 and death occurred on 15 September 2020 so Boris survived three years after the date of the gift but not four years. Taper relief is therefore 20% so 80% of the tax is chargeable £70,000 × 80% = £56,000.

(e) This was a CLT so there is lifetime tax to deduct. The tax due is therefore £56,000 – £15,000 = £41,000.

Illustration 9: Death tax on lifetime gifts proforma

Death tax

	£	£
Gross CLT/PET		X
Less nil band remaining: Nil band on death	325,000	
Less GCTs in 7 years before gift	(X)	
Nil band remaining		(X)
		X
Tax @ 40%		IHT
Less taper relief		
% × IHT		(X)
		X
Less lifetime tax (on CLT)		(X)
Death tax due		X

Activity 4: Death tax on lifetime gifts 1

Mr Fowler made the following gifts during his lifetime:

3 March 2013	Gift to nephew	£40,000
14 October 2017	Gift to granddaughter on her marriage	£158,000
23 November 2018	Gift to son	£210,000

He died on 13 September 2020.

Required

State the death tax payable on each of the gifts and who it is paid by:

(a) **Gift to nephew**

   The tax is   £ [   ]

   The tax is paid by [▼]

   Picklist:

   Mr Fowler's estate
   nephew
   nobody

(b) Gift to granddaughter

The tax is £ [_____]

The tax is paid by [_____ ▼]

Picklist:

granddaughter
Mr Fowler's estate
nobody

(c) Gift to son

The tax is £ [_____]

The tax is paid by [_____ ▼]

Picklist:

Mr Fowler's estate
nobody
son

Activity 5: Death tax on lifetime gifts 2

Mr Raymond made the following gifts during his lifetime:

13 May 2015	Gift to daughter	£130,000
23 August 2015	Gift into a trust	£334,000

He died on 7 June 2020.

The lifetime tax was as follows:

(i)

		£
PET 13.5.15:		
Gift		130,000
– AE 15/16		(3,000)
– AE 14/15		(3,000)
PET		124,000

No lifetime tax due on PETs

(ii)

	£	£
CLT 23.8.15		
Gift		334,000
– AEs (all used)		Nil
CLT		334,000
Less nil band at gift	325,000	
Less GCTs in 7 years before gift	(–)	(325,000)
		9,000
Tax @ 25% ($^{20}/_{80}$)		2,250

Gross chargeable transfer is £336,250 (334,000 + 2,250).

State the death tax payable on each of the gifts and who it is paid by:

(a) Gift to daughter

The tax is £ [   ]

The tax is paid by [▼]

Picklist:

daughter
Mr Raymond's estate
nobody

(b) Gift to trust

The tax is £ [   ]

The tax is paid by [▼]

Picklist:

Mr Raymond's estate
nobody
trustees

Activity 6: Death tax on lifetime gifts 3

Marco made the following gifts during his lifetime:

| 15 September 2012 | Gross chargeable transfer | £186,000 |
| 23 August 2015 | Gift to daughter | £164,000 |

He died on 23 November 2020.

Required

The tax paid by his daughter is   £ ⬚

---

4 Death tax paid on assets owned at death (death estate)

The final stage is to calculate tax payable on the assets owned at death, the death estate.

Step 1

Identify the value of the death estate.

Step 2

Apply exemptions – remember that assets transferred to a spouse/civil partner and gifts to charities and political parties are always exempt. The other exemptions we considered will not apply on death, they are for lifetime transfers only.

Step 3

Key term

> Identify if a **residence nil rate band** (RNRB) applies, and deduct that. An estate is entitled to a RNRB (introduced from 6 April 2017) if it contains a home (or a share of a home) which is being left to direct descendants (ie. children and grandchildren, or their spouses or civil partners).

The RNRB available for an estate is the lower of:

- The value of the home being left to direct descendants, and
- The maximum threshold which is £175,000 in 2020/21.

Step 4

Identify **all** transfers (PETs and CLTs) made in the seven years prior to death. Deduct the gross value of these transfers from the nil rate band.

Step 5

If there is any nil rate band remaining deduct it from the value of the death estate. Apply the death rate at 40%. The tax is paid out of the value in the estate so the final party named in the will (**the residuary legatee**) effectively pays the tax as they will receive a smaller legacy as a result of the tax payment. The tax is actually paid over by the **executors**, the people responsible for distributing the assets in accordance with the terms of the will.

4.1 Calculating the death estate

Illustration 10: The death estate proforma

X Deceased

Date of death .....

	£	£
Freehold property	X	
Less mortgage and accrued interest	(X)	
		X
Stocks and shares		X
Insurance policy proceeds		X
Leasehold property		X
Cars		X
Personal chattels		X
Debts due to deceased		X
Cash		X
Less: debts due from deceased		(X)
funeral expenses		(X)
Less exempt transfers		(X)
CHARGEABLE ESTATE		X

Note. Debts may only be deducted if they are legally enforceable so for example a simple (gratuitous) promise to pay a friend or relative would not be deductible.

Reasonable funeral expenses would also include the cost of a gravestone.

Illustration 11: The death estate

Zack died on 19 June 2020.

Zack's assets at the date of his death consisted of the following.

- 10,000 shares in A plc valued at £8,525

- Cash in bank £114,280

- His home, a freehold property valued at £150,000 subject to a repayment mortgage of £45,000

Zack's debts due at the date of his death were as follows:

- Electricity £150
- Council tax £300

Zack had also told his daughter on 10 June 2020 that he would pay £1,000 towards the cost of her summer holiday and that he would pay her this amount on 1 July 2020.

Zack's executors paid reasonable funeral expenses of £2,000 (including the cost of a gravestone) on 1 September 2020.

Zack's death estate for IHT purposes is as follows:

	£	£
A plc shares		8,525
Cash in bank		114,280
Freehold property	150,000	
Less repayment mortgage	(45,000)	
		105,000
Gross estate		227,805
Less: debts and funeral expenses		
electricity (incurred for consideration)	150	
council tax (imposed by law)	300	
amount towards holiday for daughter (gratuitous promise)	0	
funeral expenses	2,000	
		(2,450)
Death estate		225,355

4.2 Calculating the tax

Illustration 12: Calculating the death tax on the estate

Zack (above) died on 19 June 2020 and had a taxable estate on death of £225,355 which he leaves in its entirety to his daughter. He made the following lifetime gifts:

15 January 2012 CLT – gross chargeable transfer £100,000

27 April 2014 – gift to wife of £30,000

20 June 2018 CLT – £50,000

25 December 2019 PET – £200,000

The inheritance tax on his estate is as follows:

	£	£
Death estate		225,355
Residence nil band (lower of £105,000 and £175,000)		(105,000)
Nil band	325,000	
Less gifts made in the previous seven years		
20 June 2018	(50,000)	
25 December 2019	(200,000)	
Taxable at 0%		(75,000)
Taxable at 40%		45,355
IHT payable		18,142

Activity 7: Tax on the death estate

Rory died on 5 May 2020, leaving an estate comprising:

- 10,000 ABC plc shares, valued at £24,400
- House worth £350,000
- Summer cottage valued at £84,000
- 1,000 XYZ Investment Ltd shares valued at £68,000

Rory had an outstanding loan of £5,750 at the time of his death.

Rory left a will directing that his son should take the shares, the house should go to his wife and the rest of his estate should go to his daughter. He had made one gross chargeable transfer during his lifetime in 2014 of £232,000.

Required

Rory's chargeable estate is	£
The tax on Rory's estate is	£

4.3 Spouses/civil partners – transfer of unused nil rate bands

If a spouse or civil partner has already died, but didn't use all of their nil band or residence nil band on death, the percentage of nil band unused can be transferred across to the other spouse (or civil partner).

This is not automatic; a claim has to be made.

Note. the RNRB was only introduced on 6 April 2017, the estate of any spouse who died before this date would not have used any RNRB as it wasn't available, therefore 100% of it is available for the second spouse's death estate.

Illustration 13: Transfer of unused nil rate band

Robert and Claudia were married for many years until the death of Robert on 10 April 2020. In his will, Robert left his share of the marital home to Claudia, and the rest of his death estate valued at £100,000 to his sister. He had made no lifetime transfers.

Claudia died on 12 January 2021 leaving the marital home, now worth £560,000 to their children, and the rest of her death estate (a balance of £900,000) to her brother. Claudia had made a chargeable lifetime transfer of £50,000 in 2016.

The inheritance tax payable on the death of Claudia, assuming that a claim is made to transfer Robert's unused nil rate bands, is calculated as follows:

	£	£
Claudia's nil rate band	325,000	
Less lifetime transfers	(50,000)	
Remaining nil band		275,000
Robert's nil band	325,000	
Nil band used by Robert at death	(100,000)	
Remaining nil band		225,000
Total nil band available on Claudia's death		500,000
Claudia's residence nil rate band		
Lower of: Value of house left to direct descendants in estate	560,000	
Maximum threshold plus Robert's unused ie £175,000 × 2	350,000	
Total residence nil rate band available on Claudia's death		350,000

The tax on Claudia's estate is therefore as follows:

	IHT £
£350,000 × 0%	0
£500,000 × 0%	0
£610,000 × 40%	244,000
£1,460,000 (£560,000 + £900,000)	244,000

Activity 8: Transfer of nil rate band

George died on 1 June 2012 with an estate valued at £400,000.

He left £250,000 of his estate to his wife Mildred and the balance to his son.

Required

The nil rate band available for Mildred on her death assuming current rates continue to apply will be £ [   ]

5 Tax planning

Consider the following tax planning points:

(a) Give assets away during lifetime. This has several benefits:

   (i)   Lifetime exemptions (annual exemption, small gifts etc) can be used.

   (ii) If the donor survives seven years there will be no death tax.

   (iii) If the donor does not survive seven years but survives at least three then taper relief will be available.

(b) Avoid giving assets to trust if possible as this will result in an immediate charge to inheritance tax.

(c) Use the nil rate band – effectively you get a new nil rate band every seven years so if you do make gifts into a trust keep them below the £325,000 threshold and if you exceed this wait seven years before making further gifts.

(d) The younger spouse/civil partner should make gifts as they are more likely to survive seven years. Assets could be transferred from the older spouse/civil partner to the younger without any adverse effects as this would be an exempt transfer. The younger could then transfer to the intended recipient.

(e) Consider skipping a generation – if you gift assets directly to your grandchildren rather than to your children then HMRC cannot tax your children on their death. If you gift to your children and they then gift to your grandchildren (their children) on their death then effectively your wealth is being taxed twice.

(f) Keep the family home until death if it is being left to a direct descendant – the residence nil rate band cannot be applied to a lifetime gift.

Chapter summary

- Inheritance tax is a tax on transfers of wealth.

- The value taxed is the loss to the donor.

- There are three stages to the inheritance tax computation that must be performed in order – lifetime tax on lifetime gifts, death tax on lifetime gifts made in the seven years prior to death and death tax on the death estate.

- There are a number of exemptions available on lifetime gifts the most important being the annual exemption.

- Transfers between spouses/civil partners are always exempt.

- A lifetime transfer is a potentially exempt transfer (PET) if it is a gift to a person or a chargeable lifetime transfer (CLT) if it is a gift to a trust.

- CLTs are taxable during lifetime. PETs are not taxable during lifetime.

- The first £325,000 of taxable gifts are taxable at 0% but this nil band is reduced by any taxable gifts made in the previous seven years.

- CLTs are taxed at rate of 20% if the donee pays the tax but at $\frac{20}{80}$ if the donor pays. If the donor pays then the gift must be grossed up by the tax paid.

- All gifts made in the seven years prior to death are chargeable to death tax at 40% including PETs. PETs made in the seven years prior to death will reduce the nil band for future gifts but PETs made more than seven years prior to death can be ignored.

- Gifts made less than seven years before death but more than three years can be tapered. Lifetime tax can be deducted from the death tax.

- Assets held at death (the death estate) are taxed at 40%. The nil rate band can be applied here but it is reduced by chargeable gifts made in the seven years prior to death.

- If someone dies without using their full nil bands any unused balance can be transferred to their spouse/civil partner on their death.

Keywords

- **Annual exemption:** The amount a taxpayer can give away in a tax year without incurring an inheritance tax charge. This is £3,000. Unused annual exemption may be carried forward into the following tax year and used after the current year's

- **Chargeable lifetime transfer:** A gift to a trust. Tax is immediately payable and also payable again if the donor dies within seven years of making the gift

- **Nil rate band:** The first £325,000 of chargeable gifts are taxed at a rate of 0%. Gifts made in the previous seven years will reduce the nil rate band

- **Residence nil rate band:** An exemption from the death estate which applies if the estate contains a home left to direct descendants

- **Potentially exempt transfer:** A gift to an individual. There is no tax payable here unless the donor dies within seven years of making the gift

BPP
LEARNING MEDIA

1 Gillian owned a 70% shareholding in R Ltd, an unquoted investment company. On 23 July 2020, she gave a 20% shareholding in R Ltd to her son. The values of shareholdings in R Ltd on 23 July 2020 were as follows:

	£
100% shareholding	600,000
70% shareholding	350,000
50% shareholding	200,000
20% shareholding	80,000

What is the diminution in value of Gillian's estate as a result of her gift on 23 July 2020?

Tick ONE box.

	✓
£150,000	
£200,000	
£80,000	
£120,000	

2 Joel and Sunita were a married couple. Sunita died in July 2012 and 65% of her nil rate band of £325,000 (2012/13) was unused. Joel died in May 2020. He had made a potentially exempt transfer (after all available exemptions) of £75,000 in August 2016. Joel left his house worth £190,000 to his son and the rest of his estate to his sister. Any relevant elections were made.

What is the total of the nil rate bands available to set against Joel's death estate?

Tick ONE box.

	✓
£811,250	
£461,250	
£536,250	
£651,250	

3 On 7 July 2015, Paul made a gross chargeable transfer (after all exemptions) of £260,000. On 19 December 2020 he gave £190,000 to a trust. Paul agreed to pay any lifetime IHT due.

How much inheritance tax will be payable by Paul on the December 2020 transfer of value?

Tick ONE box.

	✓
£28,250	
£31,250	
£29,750	
£23,800	

4 Donald made the following transactions in the tax year 2020/21:

(1) A gift of £2,000 to his grand-daughter on the occasion of her marriage.

(2) A sale of a vase to his friend, Alan, for £1,000 which both Donald and Alan believed to be the market value of the vase. The vase was later valued by an auction house as worth £20,000 at the date of the sale.

Ignoring the annual exemption, what is the total value of potentially exempt transfers made by Donald as a result of these gifts?

Tick ONE box.

	✓
£21,000	
Nil	
£2,000	
£19,000	

5   Kirstin gave shares worth £150,000 to a trust on 15 September 2013 and shares worth £600,000 to her brother on 10 July 2017. Kirstin died on 23 October 2020. These figures are stated after claiming the relevant annual exemptions.

What is the inheritance tax payable on Kirstin's death in relation to her lifetime transfers?

Tick ONE box.

	✓
£170,000	
£88,000	
£136,000	
£132,160	

6   Mary made the following gifts in the tax year 2020/21:

(1)   £1,000 on the first day of each month for nine months to her grandson to pay university living expenses. Mary used income surplus to her living requirements to make these payments.

(2)   £100 to her grand-nephew on his birthday and a further £250 to the same grand-nephew as a Christmas gift.

Ignoring the annual exemption, what is the total value of potentially exempt transfers made by Mary as a result of these gifts?

Tick ONE box.

	✓
£9,350	
£100	
£9,000	
£350	

7 Daniel owned all 1,000 shares in Q Ltd, an unquoted investment company. On 10 October 2020, Daniel gave 300 of his shares in Q Ltd to his daughter. The values of the shares on 10 October 2020 were as follows:

% shareholding	Value per share £
76–100	150
51–75	120
26–50	90
1–25	30

What is the diminution in value of Daniel's estate as a result of his gift on 10 October 2020?

Tick ONE box.

	✓
£60,000	
£27,000	
£66,000	
£84,000	

8 Susanna died on 19 November 2020. Her estate consisted of an investment property worth £200,000 (on which there was a repayment mortgage of £60,000) and investments and cash totalling £350,000. Her executors paid funeral expenses of £5,000. Susanna left a cash legacy of £100,000 to her husband and the residue of her estate to her son and daughter. Susanna had not made any lifetime transfers of value.

How much inheritance tax will be payable on Susanna's estate?

£ _____

9 Rodney died on 13 August 2020. In his will he left £200 in cash to each of his 5 nephews, investments held in ISAs valued at £350,000 to his daughter, and the residue of his estate, which amounted to £520,000, including his share in the marital home, to his wife.

What is the chargeable estate for inheritance purposes?

£ _____

10 Ruth made a chargeable lifetime transfer of £750,000 on 18 June 2020. The tax rate used was 20/80. Ruth died on 10 July 2020.

Who pays the lifetime tax and the death tax?

Tick ONE box.

Lifetime tax	Death tax	✓
Ruth	Ruth's estate	
Ruth	Trustees	
Trustees	Ruth's estate	
Trustees	Trustees	

The tax and ethical framework 10

Learning outcomes

1	Analyse the theories, principles and rules that underpin taxation systems
1.1	Evaluate the objectives and functions of taxation • The principles underpinning tax systems • The features of tax systems, including tax bases and structures • How to compare progressive, regressive and proportional tax criteria used in evaluating a tax system
1.2	Differentiate between tax planning, tax avoidance and tax evasion • Definitions of tax planning, tax avoidance and tax evasion • Ethical implications of avoidance and evasion • Requirements to report suspected tax evasion under current legislation
1.3	Discuss the roles and responsibilities of a taxation practitioner • AAT's expectations of its members, as set out in the *AAT Code of Professional Ethics* • Principles of confidentiality, as applied in taxation situations • How to deal with clients and third parties
1.4	Discuss residence and domicile • The definitions of residence and domicile • The impact that each of these has on the taxation position of a UK taxpayer

Assessment context

Task 1 of the AAT sample assessment 1 required you to explain the steps that you would take in a situation where you were presented with evidence that one of your clients was in receipt of income that they had failed to advise you of. This was a 10-mark written task that would be human marked in the live assessment.

Task 1 of the AAT sample assessment 2 required you to explain the terms tax planning, tax avoidance and tax evasion, and give an example of each. This was a 10-mark written task that would be human marked in the live assessment.

Qualification context

Professional ethics are vital for a member of the AAT. The tax knowledge in this chapter is useful background in the *Business Tax* course.

Business context

A tax practitioner needs to know the duties and obligations that they owe to their client, the tax authorities and the Government.

A tax practitioner needs to know and understand the detailed tax rules.

Chapter overview

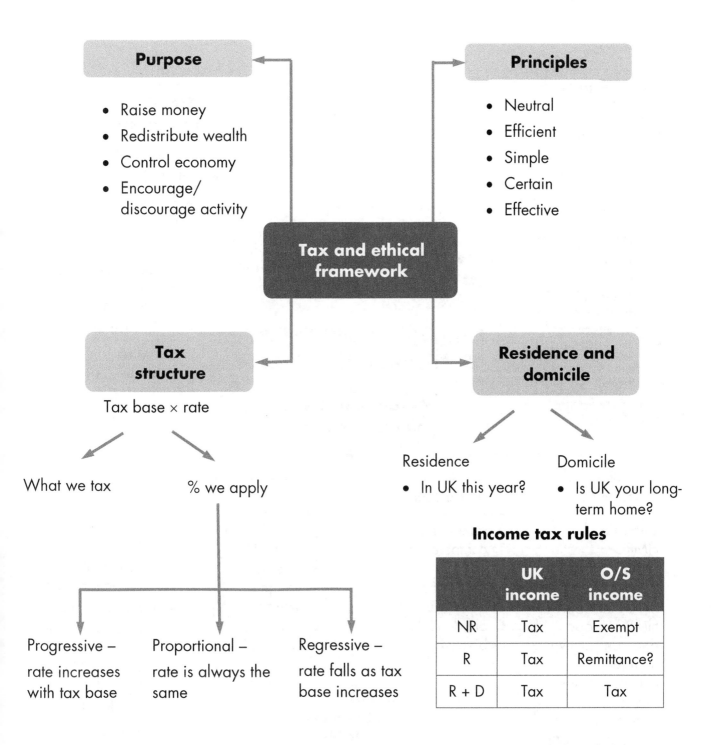

Purpose

- Raise money
- Redistribute wealth
- Control economy
- Encourage/discourage activity

Principles

- Neutral
- Efficient
- Simple
- Certain
- Effective

Tax and ethical framework

Tax structure

Tax base × rate

- What we tax
- % we apply

Residence and domicile

Residence
- In UK this year?

Domicile
- Is UK your long-term home?

Progressive – rate increases with tax base

Proportional – rate is always the same

Regressive – rate falls as tax base increases

Income tax rules

	UK income	O/S income
NR	Tax	Exempt
R	Tax	Remittance?
R + D	Tax	Tax

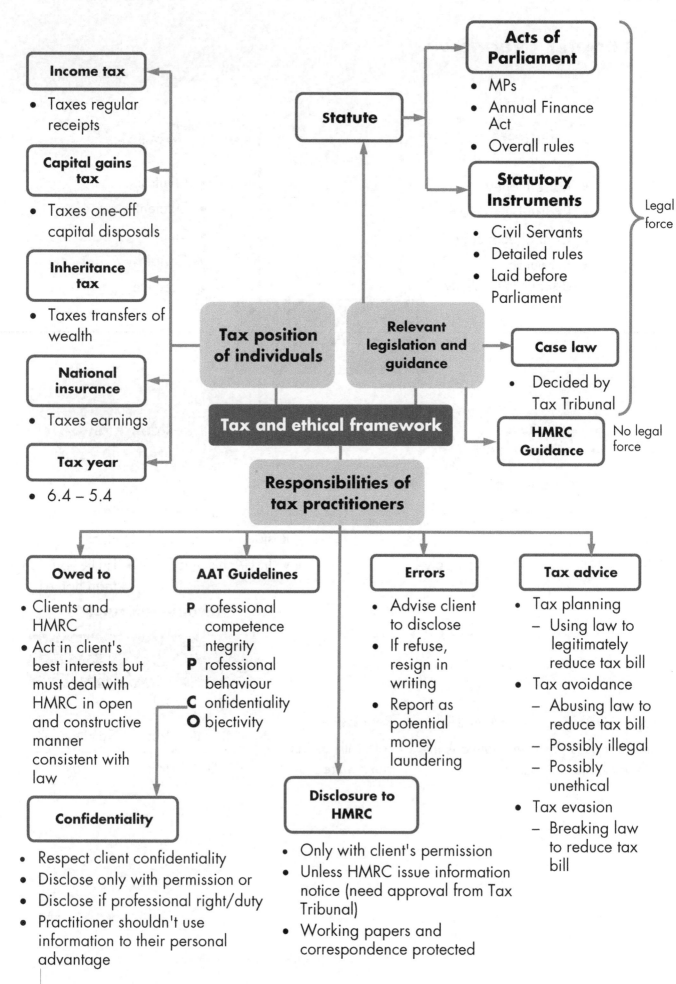

Tax and ethical framework

Tax position of individuals

Income tax
- Taxes regular receipts

Capital gains tax
- Taxes one-off capital disposals

Inheritance tax
- Taxes transfers of wealth

National insurance
- Taxes earnings

Tax year
- 6.4 – 5.4

Relevant legislation and guidance

Statute

Acts of Parliament
- MPs
- Annual Finance Act
- Overall rules

Statutory Instruments
- Civil Servants
- Detailed rules
- Laid before Parliament

Legal force

Case law
- Decided by Tax Tribunal

HMRC Guidance — No legal force

Responsibilities of tax practitioners

Owed to
- Clients and HMRC
- Act in client's best interests but must deal with HMRC in open and constructive manner consistent with law

AAT Guidelines
- **P** rofessional competence
- **I** ntegrity
- **P** rofessional behaviour
- **C** onfidentiality
- **O** bjectivity

Errors
- Advise client to disclose
- If refuse, resign in writing
- Report as potential money laundering

Tax advice
- Tax planning
  - Using law to legitimately reduce tax bill
- Tax avoidance
  - Abusing law to reduce tax bill
  - Possibly illegal
  - Possibly unethical
- Tax evasion
  - Breaking law to reduce tax bill

Confidentiality
- Respect client confidentiality
- Disclose only with permission or
- Disclose if professional right/duty
- Practitioner shouldn't use information to their personal advantage

Disclosure to HMRC
- Only with client's permission
- Unless HMRC issue information notice (need approval from Tax Tribunal)
- Working papers and correspondence protected

Introduction

This chapter introduces you to some key background principles which will underlie all of your taxation studies, and ethical principles that are vital to a tax practitioner working in the real world.

1 The objectives and functions of taxation

1.1 The purpose of taxation

Governments will collect taxation for a number of reasons:

The primary reason will be **to raise money for the Government** to use in **providing infrastructure** such as roads **and services** such as the National Health Service.

Taxes can also be used as a means of **redistributing wealth** from rich to poor, ensuring poorer people have an adequate standard of living and access to vital services.

Taxes can also be used to **control the economy**. In times of recession, taxes are cut to encourage people to spend money and stimulate the economy. In times of boom, taxes are raised to discourage people from spending money and causing the economy to overheat and crash.

Taxes can also be used to **encourage and discourage various types of activity**. For example, the Government wants us to save for our old age so we are not dependent on the state so paying into a pension saves you tax. Smoking will be harmful for you in the long run causing costs to the National Health Service so the Government taxes it. This results in higher prices for consumers discouraging them from smoking.

1.2 Principles of taxation

There are a number of principles that should be considered when creating a tax system:

Generally, taxation should be **neutral** if possible. This means that the tax paid should not discourage or encourage taxpayers from taking a particular course of action. Also the Government should not favour one business activity over another so different industries should not pay tax at different rates. Clearly this will not always be the case. As noted above often the Government will use the tax system to influence the decisions people make.

Taxes should be **efficient**. This means that the administration of the tax system should not cost an excessive amount, otherwise the Government will lose much of the revenue it raises before it has the chance to use it for the purposes for which it was collected.

Taxes should be **simple** and **certain**. This means that they should be easy to understand and calculate. If the rules are not simple, taxpayers may be exposed to penalties because they have misunderstood the rules and not paid the right amount of tax. This would seem unfair if it was no fault of their own. Conversely, complex tax rules provide greater scope for avoidance (see later). If tax rules are not certain then people cannot adequately plan their financial affairs. For example, how could you decide whether to accept either a pay rise or use of a company car if you did not know how each would be taxed?

Taxes should be **effective**, collecting the money the Government needs when they need it.

Taxes should be perceived as being **fair** or **equitable**. This is normally understood to mean that they should be based on the taxpayer's ability to pay.

1.3 Tax bases and structures

The **tax structure** of the country is essentially the way the tax system has been set up. At a simple level an amount (**the tax base**) will be taxed by multiplying it by a percentage (**the tax rate**). Governments will clearly have a lot of leeway to decide what is to be taxed and at what rate.

We have studied the following UK taxes:

Key term

Income tax The tax base here is income received by individuals (receipts which are expected to recur, for example the monthly receipt of a salary or rent received from an investment property). The tax rate will vary with the levels of income.

Capital gains tax The tax base here is capital gains made by individuals (one-off profits on disposal of capital items, for example the sale of an investment property). The tax rate will vary with levels of income and the size of the gain.

National Insurance The tax base here is earnings made by an individual from employment or self-employment (we are only concerned with employment rules in this module). The tax rate will vary with levels of earnings.

Inheritance tax The tax base here is the value of wealth transferred by an individual. The tax rate varies depending on the amount of wealth transferred.

1.4 The rate of tax

When setting the rate of tax a government can choose between three different models:

Key term

Progressive The tax rate here increases as the amount to be taxed (tax base) increases. This is usually perceived as being the fairest model.

Regressive The tax rate here decreases as the amount to be taxed increases. This is usually perceived as being the unfairest model.

Proportional The tax rate is always the same regardless of the level of income.

Most tax rates in the UK are progressive. For example, with income tax, no tax is paid on the first £12,500 of income then if the income is **non-savings,** income tax is paid at 20%, then 40% then 45% as income increases.

Value Added Tax (VAT) (a tax not on your syllabus but you will have had experience of this in your day-to-day life) appears to be proportional as everyone pays 20% regardless of their level of income. However, there is an argument that this is a regressive tax as it is only levied on expenditure and poorer people will spend a greater proportion of their income than richer people. Poorer people are therefore paying a greater proportion of their income out as tax than richer people.

Note that you will be provided with much of this information in the reference material available in the assessment (and in the back of this Course Book).

2 The UK tax system

2.1 Her Majesty's Revenue & Customs

Taxes in the UK are administered by **Her Majesty's Revenue & Customs (HMRC)**.

2.2 Tax year

Key term

Tax year This runs from 6 April to the following 5 April. It is also known as the **fiscal year** or the **year of assessment**. Tax is calculated on the income earned, wealth transferred and gains realised in the tax year.

The year of assessment 2020/21 runs from 6 April 2020 to 5 April 2021.

Some taxpayers will have to complete a tax return and pay tax under the self-assessment system. However, most taxpayers will have all their tax deducted at source. There is therefore no requirement for these taxpayers to complete a return.

2.3 Legislation

The Government creates tax law. Tax laws consist of:

(a) **Acts of Parliament** – These are created via MPs debating in Parliament. There are a number of Acts that give the main rules for each of the UK taxes. These are updated each year by the annual **Finance Act**. Periodically they will be rewritten from scratch.

(b) **Statutory Instruments (SI)** – These are created by civil servants acting on behalf of the **Chancellor of the Exchequer**. They include the detailed rules for the operation of UK taxes. An SI will be laid before Parliament and becomes law if no objections are raised.

2.4 Case law

A taxpayer and HMRC may disagree over the interpretation of the **legislation**. Such disagreements will be heard by the **Tax Tribunal**. Once a decision has been reached, this has the force of law so all future taxpayers and HMRC officers must follow the decision.

2.5 HMRC guidance

HMRC publishes a range of guidance material to advise taxpayers as to how it interprets the law, for example statements of practice and extra statutory concessions. HMRC guidance does not have legal force and could be challenged in court by a taxpayer.

3 Residence and domicile

Taxpayers are taxed in the UK with reference to their residence and domicile status.

3.1 Definitions

Key term

> **Residence** This is effectively a short-term test – is the taxpayer in the UK in a particular tax year?
>
> **Domicile** This is a long-term test – is the UK the taxpayer's real home?

It is relatively easy to lose or gain residence by coming to the UK or leaving it.

Generally, an individual is **resident** in the UK if they are present in the UK for more than half the tax year, their only home is in the UK or they carry out full time work in the UK.

Domicile is a general law concept. If you were born in the UK, have lived here for most of your life, or are now living here permanently, this is a good indication that you are domiciled in the UK. However, many situations are more complex than this. There are three types of domicile: domicile of origin, domicile of dependence, and domicile of choice. You normally acquire a domicile of origin from your father when you are born. This means that even if you are born in the UK, you may not necessarily be UK domiciled. Until the age of 16, your domicile will follow the person on whom you are legally dependent, for example your father. You have the legal capacity to acquire a new domicile at the age of 16. However, to acquire a domicile of choice you must leave your current country of domicile and settle in another country permanently or indefinitely.

There is also a concept of **deemed domicile**. If you are not domiciled in the UK under English common law, you are treated as domiciled in the UK for all tax purposes if either condition A or condition B is met.

If you meet the deemed domicile rules you will be assessed on your world wide income.

Condition A

The individual:

- Was born in the UK;
- Domicile of origin was UK and
- Was resident in the UK for 2017/2018 or later years.

Condition B

The individual has been UK resident for at least 15 of the 20 years immediately before the tax year.

3.2 Impact of the rules

3.2.1 Income tax

A taxpayer who is resident and domiciled in the UK pays tax in the UK on their worldwide income. This means they pay tax on all their income regardless of where it is earned.

A taxpayer who is resident but not domiciled in the UK automatically pays tax in the UK on the income earned in the UK. Any income earned outside the UK may be subject to the remittance basis, this means it is only taxed in the UK if the taxpayer brings it into the UK. If the income is left outside the UK it is not subject to UK tax. The rules on claiming the remittance basis are complex and outside the scope of your assessment.

A non-resident individual only pays tax on income made in the UK. Income earned overseas cannot be taxed in the UK regardless of whether it is brought into the UK or not.

> **Illustration 1: Residence rules**
>
> Alan and Marie-Claude live in France. They both come to work in the UK. Alan was originally born in the UK and his father was domiciled in the UK, and has retained ownership of his house in the UK. Marie-Claude was born in France (her parents were domiciled in France) and has always lived there.
>
> Both receive rental income from letting out their French homes while they are working in the UK. The rental income is left in a French bank.
>
> Both Alan and Marie-Claude will pay tax in the UK on their UK employment income.
>
> Alan will have to pay tax on the French rental income in the UK because he is resident in the UK (he works in the UK) and domiciled in the UK (he was born in the UK and has retained his house in the UK).
>
> Marie-Claude will probably not pay tax in the UK on the French rental income because although she is resident in the UK (she works in the UK) she is domiciled in France (she was born there and does not appear to have made steps to make the UK her permanent home). She will therefore be subject to the remittance basis and will only be taxed on the overseas income if she brings it into the UK.

3.2.2 Income tax summary

	UK income	Overseas income
Not resident	Taxable	Exempt
Resident	Taxable	Remittance basis available
Resident and domiciled/ deemed domiciled	Taxable	Taxable

3.2.3 Other taxes

We have considered the impact of residence and domicile on other taxes in the relevant chapters of this Course Book.

4 Tax planning, tax avoidance and tax evasion

Nobody wants to pay tax! As a tax adviser your client will expect you to help them reduce their tax bill if possible. This is a complex area for an adviser because there are legal ways to reduce a tax bill encouraged by the Government and illegal ways prevented by law and a grey area between the two.

Clearly as an adviser you should be helping your client but not breaking the law. These complex areas are addressed in the *Professional conduct in relation to taxation* section that follows.

4.1 Tax planning

This is perfectly legal and involves using the rules to reduce your tax bill in the way that they were intended. For example paying into a pension scheme would reduce your tax bill.

The Government accepts that everyone is entitled to structure their financial affairs in such a way that their tax bill is legally reduced to as little as possible.

4.2 Tax avoidance

On the face of it this appears permissible but is fraught with legal and ethical complications. It involves using the rules to reduce your tax bill in a way not intended by the Government. You may not be breaking the law but you may be 'bending the rules' or exploiting 'a loophole'. By this we mean the actual words used in the relevant tax legislation may appear to permit you do something but it is clear that this was not the intention of the Government when the law was written.

The taxpayer's reading of the law could be challenged by HMRC in court. If the judge does not agree with the taxpayer's interpretation then the avoidance will fail and the perpetrator will have to pay the avoided tax.

Often a taxpayer will have to engage in 'artificial transactions' when pursuing tax avoidance. This means that they are doing something purely to obtain a tax advantage, there can be no other reason for the transaction.

In the UK such artificial transactions can be set aside by the Government making the tax avoidance ineffective.

Activity 1: Tax avoidance?

Dave is self-employed. His wife Doris works for him. Dave pays her £11,000 a year for the work she does.

Required

Discuss whether or not you think this represents tax avoidance.

Solution

Finally there is the moral/ethical issue. A judge may rule that the tax avoidance is legally effective and HMRC may not be able to prove it represents an artificial transaction. In this case the avoidance will work and the taxpayer will save tax but this doesn't make it right.

 Real life example

If you do an internet search for 'celebrity tax avoiders' you will find some interesting stories!

4.3 Tax evasion

This is illegal. This involves clearly breaking the tax law, for example failing to declare the profits of a business.

4.4 Summary

These distinctions are not always clear cut and so it is best to see this as a spectrum. It is not always obvious where tax planning ends and mild tax avoidance begins or the point at which aggressive potentially illegal tax avoidance becomes illegal tax evasion.

5 Professional conduct in relation to taxation

These are the rules that govern the relationship between a tax adviser and their client and HMRC.

The detailed rules are available to you in your assessment and are included in the *Reference material and tax tables* at the back of this Course Book. We recommend that you read these carefully. As they are available to you in the assessment you don't need to learn this information word for word but it is important that you remember the gist of it and know where to find the various sections.

To summarise, a tax practitioner should act in the best interests of their client; however, they must deal with HMRC staff in an open and constructive manner consistent with the law.

A tax adviser must follow the fundamental principles, particularly that of confidentiality.

A tax return may be prepared by an adviser but ultimately it is the taxpayer's responsibility and must be approved by the taxpayer before being submitted. The adviser should make this clear to the taxpayer and highlight any areas where they have had to exercise their judgement when preparing the return.

Providing tax advice is an ethically complex area for an adviser.

If a tax adviser learns of an error, omission or a failure to file a tax return, the adviser should bring this to the taxpayer's attention and request permission to disclose this to HMRC.

If the taxpayer refuses to disclose, then the adviser should notify the taxpayer in writing that they are unable to continue to act for them.

If the tax adviser works in an organisation they must report this to their Money Laundering Reporting Officer or, if the adviser is a sole practitioner directly to the National Crime Agency (NCA). The taxpayer should not be advised that a report has been made.

The adviser should consider whether to advise HMRC that previous information cannot be relied upon and consider how to answer any requests from a potential new adviser.

Usually, a practitioner would only disclose information to HMRC with the taxpayer's permission. In limited circumstances though, HMRC may gain access to information without the client's permission. This is a complex area.

Activity 2: Irregularities

You act as tax adviser for Frank who is self-employed. Frank is currently divorcing his wife Vivien. You receive a large parcel from Vivien containing some significant sales invoices that Vivien says Frank has deliberately excluded from his accounting profits.

Required

What action should you take?

Solution

Assessment focus point

In the assessment, the ethics question will be assessed as a written task. The key to written tasks is:

- Short sentences – get to the point

- Think about the 'flow' of your answer eg if you are asked about the steps you should take, show them in order

- Make use of the reference material provided to you in the exam (reproduced at the back of this Course Book), but remember to apply it to the scenario

See the section in the Skills Bank on answering written questions.

Chapter summary

- Governments collect taxation to raise finance, redistribute wealth, control the economy and encourage or discourage certain activities.

- Taxes should be neutral, efficient, simple, certain, effective and fair.

- The tax structure depends upon the tax base used and the tax rate applied.

- Individuals may have to pay income tax, capital gains tax, National Insurance and/or inheritance tax.

- Tax rates may be progressive, regressive or proportional.

- HMRC is responsible for the administration of tax.

- The tax year runs from 6 April in one year to the 5 April in the next year.

- Some of the rules governing tax are laid down in legislation, while some are laid down in case law.

- HMRC provides guidance about how tax law works.

- Residence and domicile are important concepts which determine how a taxpayer is taxed on UK and overseas income and assets.

- Tax evasion is illegal, tax planning is legal and tax avoidance may or may not be technically legal but is sometimes ethically wrong.

- Tax practitioners have responsibilities to their clients and to HMRC.

- The tax return is ultimately the client's responsibility.

- Providing tax advice is an ethically complex area.

- The ethical guideline of confidentiality means that a client's tax affairs should not be discussed with third parties without the client's permission unless there is a legal right or obligation for the adviser to disclose the information.

- Tax practitioners may be required to produce information to HMRC.

- A tax practitioner must cease to act for a client who refuses to disclose an error or omission to HMRC, and must make a money laundering report.

Keywords

- **Acts of Parliament:** Laws produced by MPs debating in Parliament

- **Capital gains tax:** Tax charged on the profits made on the disposal of capital items

- **Case law:** Decisions of the Tax Tribunal about the interpretation of tax statutes which serve as a further source of tax law

- **Domicile:** A long-term test to identify whether the UK is a taxpayer's real home

- **Her Majesty's Revenue & Customs (HMRC):** Responsible for the administration of tax

- **Income tax:** Tax charged on money a taxpayer regularly receives

- **Inheritance tax:** Tax charged on transfer of wealth

- **Legislation:** Laws created by the Government. These include Acts of Parliament and Statutory Instruments

- **National Insurance:** Tax paid on earnings from employment or self-employment

- **Progressive tax:** Tax rate increases as the tax base increases

- **Proportional tax:** Tax rate stays the same as the tax base changes

- **Regressive tax:** Tax rate decreases as the tax base increases

- **Residence:** A short-term test to identify whether someone is present in the UK for tax purposes in a tax year

- **Statutory instrument:** Laws produced by civil servants acting on behalf of the Chancellor of the Exchequer

- **Tax avoidance:** Using the tax legislation in a way that was not intended to reduce tax liabilities. May or may not be technically illegal but sometimes ethically wrong

- **Tax base:** The amount that will be taxed

- **Tax evasion:** Breaking the law and not paying the correct amount of tax

- **Tax planning:** Taking advantage of legal means by which a taxpayer may reduce their tax bill

- **Tax rate:** The percentage applied to the tax base

- **Tax structure:** The way the tax system has been organised

- **The tax year (fiscal year or year of assessment):** The 12-month period that runs from 6 April in one year to 5 April in the next year. Thus the tax year 2020/21 runs from 6 April 2020 to 5 April 2021

1   **Identify whether the statement below is true or false.**

Statement	True ✓	False ✓
All taxpayers are sent a tax return each year by HM Revenue & Customs.		

2   The tax administration within the UK is undertaken by:

Tick ONE box.

	✓
The Chancellor of the Exchequer	
Companies House	
HM Revenue & Customs	
Members of Parliament	

3   **Indicate with ticks which TWO of the following have the force of law.**

	✓
Acts of Parliament	
HMRC statements of practice	
Statutory Instruments	
Extra statutory concessions	

4   When is a tax practitioner not bound by the ethical guidelines of client confidentiality?

Tick ONE box.

	✓
When in a social environment	
When discussing client affairs with third parties with the client's proper and specific authority	
When reading documents relating to a client's affairs in public places	
When preparing tax returns	

5 Who should a sole practitioner make a report to if they suspect a client of money laundering?

Tick ONE box.

	✓
HMRC	
Nearest police station	
National Crime Agency	
Tax Tribunal	

6 Cornelius is an acquaintance of your client, Ruby, as they have similar jobs in similar sized companies. He knows that Ruby was made redundant recently. He is facing redundancy himself and would like to know how much redundancy money Ruby received so that he can compare this to the figure his company is offering him.

State how you should reply to his request for this information, clearly justifying your reply.

7 An ISA is a special bank account where cash may be saved and any interest earned is not subject to tax. David invests his redundancy money in an ISA. David is engaged in:

Tick ONE box.

	✓
Tax planning	
Tax avoidance	
Tax evasion	
Not possible to say until decided by a judge	

8   In country Z income tax is levied at a flat rate of 10% on all earnings. The tax rate is:

Tick ONE box.

Progressive	
Regressive	
Proportional	
Equitable	

9   James leaves the UK to work abroad for five years. He intends to return to the UK and stay there once the job ends. James's UK status is:

Tick ONE box.

Not resident or domiciled	
Not resident but domiciled	
Resident but not domiciled	
Resident and domiciled	

10 Pierre comes to visit the UK for the first time for a three-month period. He does not work in the UK during this period. He deposits money in a UK bank account and earns interest. He also receives rental income overseas and brings some of it into the UK. Pierre will be:

Tick ONE box.

Taxed on all of his income in the UK regardless as to where it is earned	
Taxed in the UK on his UK income and income brought into the UK from overseas	
Taxed in the UK only on his UK income	
Not taxed in the UK	

Activity answers

CHAPTER 1 Taxable income

Activity 1: Taxable and exempt income

	Exempt income £	Non-savings income £	Savings income £	Dividend income £
Exempt income				
ISA dividend	900			
Non–savings income				
Rent		6,000		
Savings income				
Building society interest			40	
Dividend income				
Non-ISA dividend				450

Activity 2: Taxable income

	Non-savings income £	Savings income £	Dividend income £	Total £
Employment income	3,000			3,000
Property income	1,000			1,000
Building society interest		3,750		3,750
Dividend income			5,000	5,000
Net income	4,000	3,750	5,000	12,750
Less personal allowance	(4,000)	(3,750)	(4,750)	(12,500)
Taxable income	nil	nil	250	250

Activity 3: Personal allowance restriction

Her personal allowance is £ 9,000

Her taxable income is £ 98,000

Workings

	£
Personal allowance	12,500
Less ½ (107,000 – 100,000) =	(3,500)
Adjusted personal allowance	9,000
Net income	107,000
Personal allowance	(9,000)
Taxable income	98,000

Activity 4: Personal allowance with personal pension payment

Her personal allowance is £ 10,000

Her taxable income is £ 97,000

Workings

	£
Net income	107,000
Less personal pension payment	(2,000)
Adjusted net income	105,000
Personal allowance	12,500
Less ½ (105,000 – 100,000)	(2,500)
Adjusted personal allowance	10,000
Net income	107,000
Personal allowance	(10,000)
Taxable income	97,000

CHAPTER 2 Calculation of income tax

Activity 1: Income tax liability

	Non-savings income £	Savings income £	Total £
Employment income	39,000		39,000
Building society interest		9,000	9,000
Net income	39,000	9,000	48,000
Personal allowance	(12,500)		(12,500)
Taxable income	26,500	9,000	35,500

Net income < £50,001 therefore £1,000 personal savings allowance available

	£
Non-savings income	
26,500 × 20%	5,300
Savings income	
1,000 × 0% (personal savings allowance)	0
8,000 × 20%	1,600
35,500	
Tax liability	6,900

Activity 2: Income tax payable

	Non-savings income £	Savings income £	Dividend income £	Total £
Employment income	125,000			125,000
Bank interest		10,000		10,000
Dividends			10,000	10,000
Net income	125,000	10,000	10,000	145,000
Personal allowance	(Nil)			(Nil)
Taxable income	125,000	10,000	10,000	145,000

Note. Total income is in excess of £125,000, so Arthur is not entitled to a personal allowance. Net income is greater than £50,000 but less than £150,000 so £500 savings allowance is available. Dividend allowance is always available.

	£
Non-savings income:	
37,500 × 20%	7,500
87,500 × 40%	35,000
125,000	
Savings income:	
500 × 0% (savings allowance)	0
9,500 × 40%	3,800
10,000	
Dividend income:	
2,000 × 0%	0
8,000 × 32.5%	2,600
10,000	
Tax liability	48,900
Less PAYE	(42,000)
Tax payable	6,900

Activity 3: Tax liability with Gift Aid donation

(a) Taxable income

£	87,500

Workings

Taxable income

	Non-savings income £
Employment income	100,000
Less personal allowance (income ≤ 100,000 ∴ no restriction)	(12,500)
Taxable income	87,500

(b) Tax liability if he does not make the donation

£	27,500

Workings

Tax liability without the donation

	£
37,500 × 20%	7,500
50,000 × 40%	20,000
87,500	
Tax liability	27,500

(c) Tax liability if he does make the donation

£	25,500

Workings

Tax liability with the donation

	£
Gross donation is 8,000 × 100/80	10,000
Basic rate extends to 10,000 + 37,500	47,500
47,500 × 20%	9,500
40,000 × 40%	16,000
87,500	
	25,500

(d) Tax saved if he does make the donation

£	4,000

Workings

Tax saving (27,500 – 25,500)	= extra 2,000
which is 20% of the gross donation	
(8,000 × 100/80 = 10,000 @ 20%)	
Total relief:	
Obtained at source: 10,000 – 8,000	2,000
Reduction in tax liability (above)	2,000
Total	4,000
ie 40% of gross donation of 10,000	

CHAPTER 3 Employment income

Activity 1: Basis of assessment

(a)

£	30,916

(b)

£	3,000

Workings

	£
Salary:	
6 April 2020 to 31 October 2020 – $^7/_{12} \times 28,000$	16,333
1 November 2021 to 5 April 2021 – $^5/_{12} \times 35,000$	14,583
Total salary	30,916
Bonus received between 6 April 2020 and 5 April 2021	3,000

Activity 2: Car and fuel benefit

(a)

£	24,420

Workings

	£
List price + accessories (60,000 + 900)	60,900
30% (W) × £60,900	18,270
Less employee contributions (12 × £100)	(1,200)
Car benefit	17,070
Plus fuel benefit (£24,500 × 30%)	7,350
Total benefit	24,420

(W)	Round down to 125	
	Relevant emissions percentage:	
	125 – 55 =	70
	Divide by 5 =	14
	Add basic	14
	Add 2% for pre 6 April 2020 car	2
		30%

(b)

£	18,315

Workings (not provided in the CBT)

	£
$30\% \times £60{,}900 \times {}^{9}/_{12}$	13,703
Less employee contributions $(9 \times £100)$	(900)
Car benefit	12,803
Add fuel benefit $(£24{,}500 \times 30\% \times {}^{9}/_{12})$	5,513
Total benefit	18,316
Alternatively 24,420 (the benefit figure from part a) $\times {}^{9}/_{12}$	18,315

Activity 3: Use and gift of employer's asset

In 2020/21, his benefit for the use of the asset is

£	150

In 2020/21, his benefit on the gift of the asset is

£	550

Workings

Use of employer's assets

(a)

	£	£
2018/19 Use: $20\% \times 1{,}000 \times {}^{6}/_{12}$	100	
2019/20 Use: $20\% \times 1{,}000$	200	
2020/21 Use: $20\% \times 1{,}000 \times {}^{9}/_{12}$	150	
		450

Gift

(b)

	£	£
2020/21 Higher of:		
• Value when given	500	
• Value when first made available for use less already		
Assessed (1,000 – 450)	550	
Benefit		550

Activity 4: Beneficial loan

The benefit calculated under the average method is   £   369

The benefit calculated under the strict method is   £   228

The taxpayer would be taxed on   £   228

Workings

Average method	£
$2.25\% \times \dfrac{40,000 + 15,000}{2}$	619
Less interest paid	(250)
Benefit	369

Alternative method (strict method)	£
£40,000 × $^3/_{12}$ (6 April – 6 July) × 2.25%	225
£15,000 × $^9/_{12}$ (7 July – 5 April) × 2.25%	253
	478
Less interest paid	(250)
Benefit	228

The taxpayer would opt for the strict method.

Activity 5: Accommodation benefit

(a) £ | nil

(b) £ | 2,750

(c) £ | 5,563

Workings

Accommodation (house bought in 1997)	£
Annual value	3,000
Less rent paid	(2,500)
	500
Add 2.25% × (175,000 – 75,000)	2,250
Taxable benefit	2,750

The property was purchased by the company less than six years before Ralph moved in so the benefit is based on cost.

Accommodation (house bought in 1992)	£
Annual value	3,000
Less rent paid	(2,500)
	500
Add 2.25% × (300,000 – 75,000)	5,063
Taxable benefit	5,563

The property was purchased by the company more than six years before Ralph moved in so the benefit is based on market value at the start of the tax year in which Ralph moved in.

Activity 6: Accommodation living expenses

If the property is 'job related' her benefit is £ | 900

If the property is not 'job related' her benefit is £ | 1,800

Workings

Living expenses	£
Lower of:	
(a) Living expenses	1,800
(b) 10% of net earnings:	
= 10% (7,000 + 2,000)	900
Taxable benefit	= 900

Activity 7: Statutory mileage

(a) If Jen's employer pays her 30p per mile she

may deduct	£1,250

Workings

Mileage calculation			£
Receives	15,000 × 0.30		4,500
Approved HMRC rates	10,000 × 0.45	4,500	
	5,000 × 0.25	1,250	(5,750)
Deductible			(1,250)

(b) If Jen's employer pays her 50p per mile she

is taxed on	£1,750

Workings

Mileage calculation		£
Receives	15,000 × 0.50	7,500
Approved HMRC rates	(as above)	(5,750)
Taxable		1,750

CHAPTER 4 Property income

Activity 1: Property income

£	6,015

Workings (not provided in the CBT)

	£
Rents	8,400
Less expenses commission	(360)
Replacement cost of equivalent single bed	(300)
Redecoration	(500)
Insurance $(^9/_{12} \times 400) + (^3/_{12} \times 500)$	(425)
Repairs to existing window	(300)
Property income	6,515
Less property losses brought forward	(500)
	6,015

Activity 2: Property allowance

	Assessable income	Make election (Y/N)
Charlotte		
(a)	Nil (Income ≤ £1,000)	N
(b)	£100 loss (Income ≤ £1,000 but better off making election and deducting expenses)	Y
Thomas		
(a)	£500 (better to make election and deduct property allowance £1,500 – £1,000)	Y
(b)	£450 (better to ignore property allowance and deduct expenses as normal)	N

CHAPTER 5 National Insurance

Activity 1: Class 1 Employee National Insurance

The Class 1 Employee National Insurance is　**£** | 4,910

Workings

Tyrone suffers Class 1 Employee contributions on his cash earnings.

Class 1 Employee contributions

$(50,000 - 9,500) \times 12\% =$ 　　4,860

$(52,500 - 50,000) \times 2\% =$ 　　 50

　　　　　　　　　　　4,910

Activity 2: Class 1 Employer National Insurance

The Class 1 Employer National Insurance is　**£** | 6,032

Workings

Class 1 Employer contributions

$(52,500 - 8,788) \times 13.8\% =$ 　6,032

Activity 3: The employment allowance

The Class 1 employer's National Insurance is　**£** | 0

Workings

	£
Employee 1: £$(18,000 - 8,788) \times 13.8\%$	1,271
Employee 2: £$(15,000 - 8,788) \times 13.8\%$	857
	2,128
Less employment allowance (maximum £4,000, restricted)	(2,128)
Employer contributions	0

Activity 4: Class 1A National Insurance

The Class 1A National Insurance payable by Taverner plc is　**£** | 890

Workings

Class 1A

$6,450 @ 13.8\% =$ 　　890

CHAPTER 6 Chargeable gains

Activity 1: Capital gain calculation

	£
Proceeds	38,500
Less selling expenses	(1,500)
Net proceeds	37,000
Less cost	(12,700)
Less legal fees on purchase	(500)
Less enhancement	(3,000)
Capital gain	20,800

Activity 2: Current year losses

Ted's net capital gain for 2020/21 before the annual exempt amount is

£	7,000

Ted has a loss to carry forward of | £ | nil |

Workings

	£
Gains 45,000 + 10,000	55,000
Less loss	(48,000)
Net capital gains	7,000
Less annual exempt amount	(12,300)
Taxable gains	Nil
The balance of the annual exempt amount is wasted.	

Activity 3: Prior year losses

Tara's net capital gain for 2020/21 before the annual exempt amount is

£	12,800

Tara has a loss to carry forward of | £ | 9,500 |

Workings

	£
Gain of 2020/21	12,800
Less annual exempt amount	(12,300)
Net gain	500
Less capital loss brought forward	(500)
Taxable gains	Nil
Losses to c/f £(10,000 – 500)	9,500

Activity 4: Computing capital gains tax payable

Mr Dunstable's capital gains tax payable is £ 1,050

Workings

	£
Capital gain	20,800
Less annual exempt amount	(12,300)
Taxable gain	8,500
Basic rate band	37,500
Taxable income	(31,000)
Basic rate band remaining	6,500

	£
Capital gains tax payable	
6,500 × 10%	650
2,000 × 20%	400
8,500	1,050

Activity 5: Part disposal

The gain on the disposal of the land is £ 4,702

The cost of the remaining land carried forward is £ 15,652

Workings

	£
Gross proceeds	10,000
Less disposal costs	(950)
Net proceeds	9,050
Cost $\dfrac{10}{10+36} \times 20,000$	(4,348)
	4,702
Cost of remaining land for future CGT calculations: =　20,000 – 4,348	15,652

Activity 6: Chattels

(a) The chargeable gain on the disposal is　£ | 5,000

Workings

Non-wasting chattel: cost ≤ £6,000, proceeds > £6,000	£
Proceeds	9,000
Less commission	(1,000)
Net proceeds	8,000
Less cost	(500)
Capital gain	7,500
$^5/_3$ (Gross proceeds – 6,000)	
= $^5/_3$ (9,000 – 6,000)	
= 5,000	
∴ take lower gain 5,000	5,000

(b) The loss on the disposal is　£ | 1,000

Workings

Non-wasting chattel: cost > £6,000, proceeds ≤ £6,000	£
Proceeds (deemed)	6,000
Less cost	(7,000)
Allowable loss	(1,000)

Activity 7: Transfers between spouses/civil partners

The chargeable gain on transfer is:

	✓
Nil	✓
£18,000	
£31,000	
£13,000	

The transfer takes place at no gain/no loss and Kate assumes the base cost of £14,000 as her cost.

£18,000 is a chargeable gain based on actual proceeds. £31,000 is a chargeable gain based on market value. £13,000 is the difference between market value and actual proceeds.

CHAPTER 7 Share disposals

Activity 1: Matching rules

	Shares
Same day	400
Next 30 days	500
Share pool	700 ß
Disposal	1,600

(1) Match with same day

	£	£
Proceeds 400/1,600 × 14,000	3,500	
Cost	(3,000)	
		500

(2) Match with next 30 days

	£	£
Proceeds 500/1,600 × 14,000	4,375	
Cost	(4,500)	
		(125)

(3) Match with share pool

	£	£
Proceeds 700/1,600 × 14,000	6,125	
Cost (W)	(2,800)	
		3,325
Net gain		3,700

(W) Share pool

	Number	Cost
15.5.02	2,200	8,800
Disposal 700/2,200 × 8,800	(700)	(2,800)
	1,500	6,000

Activity 2: Share pool

Matching rules: The shares were all acquired prior to the date of disposal so they are all in the share pool.

	£
Proceeds	14,000
Cost (Working)	(4,500)
Gain	9,500

Working: Share pool

	Number	Cost £
January 1985		
Purchase	3,000	5,000
February 1987		
Purchase	1,000	4,000
	4,000	9,000
May 2020		
Disposal 2,000/4,000 × 9,000	(2,000)	(4,500)
	2,000	4,500

Activity 3: Bonus and rights issues

Matching rules: All bought prior to date of disposal so all from share pool.

Gain

	£
Proceeds	15,000
Less cost (Working)	(10,139)
Gain	4,861

Working: Share pool

	Number	Cost £
1.10.95	10,000	15,000
11.9.99 acquisition	2,000	5,000
	12,000	20,000
1.2.00 1:2 rights @ £2.75	6,000	16,500
	18,000	36,500
5.9.05 2:1 bonus	36,000	–
	54,000	36,500
14.10.20 sale 15,000/54,000 × 36,500	(15,000)	(10,139)
	39,000	26,361

CHAPTER 8 Private residence relief

Activity 1: Private residence relief

The gain on the disposal of his house is   £   69,811

Workings

Periods of absence	Occ. (mths)	Non-occ. (mths)	
1.4.94–31.3.95			
(occupation)	12		
1.4.95–31.3.97			
(working overseas)	24		
1.4.97–31.3.00			
(up to 4 years working in UK)	36		

Periods of absence	Occ. (mths)	Non-occ. (mths)	
1.4.00–30.6.01			
(occupation)	15		
1.7.01–31.12.19			
(no deemed occupation as property not reoccupied)		222	
1.1.20–30.9.20			
(Last nine months)	9		
	96	222	= 318

Capital gain	£
Gain	100,000
Less private residence relief 100,000 × 96/318	(30,189)
Gain	69,811

CHAPTER 9 Inheritance tax

Activity 1: Diminution of value

What is the value of the gift for inheritance tax purposes? **£ 170,000**

Workings

	£
Value before transfer	370,000
Value after transfer	(200,000)
Transfer of value for IHT	170,000

Activity 2: Calculating lifetime tax – CLTs only

(a) The trust agrees to pay the tax

The tax payable is **£ 23,200**

The gross chargeable transfer is **£ 331,000**

Workings

		£
Gift (CLT)		337,000
AE: 2020/21		(3,000)
2019/20 b/f		(3,000)
Net gift after exemptions		331,000
Nil band left	325,000	
Less GCTs in previous 7 years before gift	(110,000)	(215,000)
		116,000
Tax at 20%		23,200

Gross chargeable transfer is £331,000.

(b) Mr Butcher pays the tax

The tax payable is   £   29,000

The gross chargeable transfer is   £   360,000

Workings

	£	£
Net gift after exemptions, as before		331,000
– Nil band left	325,000	
Less GCTs in 7 years before gift	(110,000)	
		(215,000)
		116,000
Tax at 25% ($^{20}/_{80}$)		29,000

Gross chargeable transfer is £360,000 (331,000 + 29,000).

Activity 3: Calculating lifetime tax – PETs and CLTs

(a) Gift to daughter

The tax is   £ | nil

(b) Gift to trust

The tax is   £ | 3,000

(c) Gift to son

The tax is   £ | nil

Workings

	£
Gift to daughter 15.3.20	
Gift	50,000
AE: 2019/20	(3,000)
2018/19 b/f	(3,000)
PET	44,000
No lifetime tax	
Gift to trust 13.8.20:	
Gift	343,000
AE: 2020/21	(3,000)
2019/20 already used	–
Gross CLT	340,000
Less nil band left	(325,000)
	15,000
Tax @ 20%	3,000
GCT £340,000	
Gift to son 19.8.20	
Gift	30,000
AE: 2020/21 and 2019/20 already used	–
PET	30,000
No lifetime tax.	

Activity 4: Death tax on lifetime gifts 1

(a) Gift to nephew

The tax is   £ | nil

The tax is paid by | nobody

(b) Gift to granddaughter

The tax is   £ | nil

The tax is paid by | nobody

(c) Gift to son

The tax is   £ | 12,600

The tax is paid by | son

Workings

Lifetime tax:

None as all transfers are PETs

Death tax:

		£	£
(a)	PET March 2013		
	– more than 7 years before death ∴ exempt		
(b)	PET October 2017:		
	Gift		158,000
	– Marriage exemption		(2,500)
	– AE 2017/18		(3,000)
	– AE 2016/17 b/f		(3,000)
	PET		149,500
	< nil band (£325,000) ∴ no tax due		
	GCT		149,500

		£	£
(c)	PET November 2018:		
	Gift		210,000
	– AE 2018/19		(3,000)
	PET		207,000
	Less nil band left	325,000	
	Less GCTs in 7 years before gift	(149,500)	
			(175,500)
			31,500
Tax @ 40%			12,600
Payable by the son			
(No taper relief as < 3 years before death)			

Activity 5: Death tax on lifetime gifts 2

(a) Gift to daughter

The tax is £ nil

The tax is paid by nobody

(b) Gift to trust

The tax is £ 30,210

The tax is paid by trustees

Workings

Death tax:

		£	£
(a)	PET 13.5.15		124,000
	< nil band at death (£325,000) ∴ no death tax		
	GCT		124,000

	£	£
(b) CLT 23.8.15		336,250
Less nil band left	325,000	
Less GCTs in 7 years before gift	(124,000)	
		(201,000)
		135,250
Tax @ 40%		54,100
Less taper relief (4–5 years) 40%		(21,640)
Less lifetime tax		(2,250)
Additional tax on death		30,210
Payable by trustees		

Activity 6: Death tax on lifetime gifts 3

The tax paid by his daughter is   £ 3,040

Workings

	£	£
15.9.12 – no further tax as donor survived 7 years		
23.8.15 Gift – PET becomes chargeable		158,000
(164,000 – 6,000)		
Less:		
Nil band remaining	325,000	
Less GCTs in 7 years before **gift**	(186,000)	
		(139,000)
		19,000
Tax @ 40%		7,600
Less taper relief: 5–6 years: 60%		(4,560)
IHT due		3,040

Activity 7: Tax on the death estate

Rory's chargeable estate is £ | 170,650

The tax on Rory's estate is £ | 31,060

Workings

Death Estate

	£	£
ABC plc shares		24,400
House	350,000	
– exempt as left to spouse	(350,000)	
Summer cottage		84,000
XYZ Ltd shares		68,000
		176,400
Less liabilities		(5,750)
Chargeable estate		170,650
Less nil band remaining		
Nil band at date of death	325,000	
– used in 7 years before death	(232,000)	
		(93,000)
		77,650
Tax @ 40%		31,060

Note. there is no residence nil rate band as the house is not left to a direct descendant.

Activity 8: Transfer of nil rate band

The nil rate band available for Mildred on Mildred's death assuming current rates continue to apply will be £ | 500,000

Workings

	£
George's estate	400,000
Less exempt transfer	(250,000)
Using up nil band	150,000
Nil rate band unused 325,000 – 150,000 = 175,000	
Mildred's own nil band	325,000
Unused nil band of husband	175,000
	500,000

The question did not mention the residence nil rate band so in the exam you should assume that it does not apply.

CHAPTER 10 The tax and ethical framework

Activity 1: Tax avoidance?

This could represent tax avoidance or tax planning. It makes sense to have Doris work for the business as by paying her £11,000 this reduces the taxable profits of the business thereby reducing Dave's tax bill. If Doris has no other income this £11,000 would be covered by her personal allowance and she would pay no tax. This appears to be effective tax planning saving them money as a couple.

However, the key issues here would be: does Doris genuinely work for the business and does Dave pay her a commercial rate?

If she does not genuinely work for the business then this is avoidance and HMRC will set the whole transaction aside. Dave will be taxed on the £11,000.

If she is paid more than Dave would have paid someone else to do the same work then this is also avoidance. HMRC will set aside the excessive amount and Dave will be taxed on it.

Activity 2: Irregularities

You should confirm the invoices are genuine and that they have been omitted from the accounts. You should then raise the matter with Frank and advise him that HMRC should be notified of the extra income, and that tax and potentially interest and penalties will be due.

If he agrees you should disclose the extra income to HMRC.

If he refuses you should advise him of the consequences first verbally and, if he still refuses, in writing. If he refuses to disclose the information you should cease to act for him and confirm this to him in writing.

You need to advise HMRC that you no longer act for him but you cannot say why as this would breach client confidentiality. You must consider making a money laundering report and consider whether you need to advise HMRC that any previous information supplied can no longer be relied on.

You need to consider carefully your response to any correspondence from a future adviser requesting whether Frank would be a suitable client.

Note. See the flowchart at 5.10 in the reference materials with regard to irregularities.

Test your learning: Answers

Chapter 1 Taxable income

1

	Non-savings income	Savings income	Dividend income
Employment income	✓		
Dividends			✓
Property income	✓		
Bank interest		✓	
Pension income	✓		
Interest on government stock		✓	

2

	Amount received £	Amount in tax return £
Building society interest	240	240
Interest on an individual savings account	40	0
Dividends	160	160
Interest from government gilts	350	350

3

	Non-savings income £	Dividend income £	Total £
Employment income	30,000		30,000
Dividends		300	300
Net income	30,000	300	30,300
Less personal allowance	(12,500)		(12,500)
Taxable income	17,500	300	17,800

Premium bond winnings are exempt from income tax.

4

	Non-savings income £	Savings income £	Total £
Property income	3,000		3,000
Building society interest		9,000	9,000
Net income	3,000	9,000	12,000
Less personal allowance	(3,000)	(9,000)	(12,000)
Taxable income	Nil	Nil	Nil

The personal allowance is deducted first from non-savings income and then from savings income. The full personal allowance was available but not used as taxable income was less than £12,500.

5

	Non-savings income £	Savings income £	Dividend income £	Total £
Employment income	112,200			112,200
Building society interest		5,000		5,000
Dividends			4,000	4,000
Net income	112,200	5,000	4,000	121,200
Less personal allowance (W)	(1,900)			(1,900)
Taxable income	110,300	5,000	4,000	119,300

Workings

	£
Net income	121,200
Less income limit	(100,000)
Excess	21,200
Personal allowance	12,500
Less half excess	(10,600)
Adjusted personal allowance	1,900

The prize is exempt from income tax.

Chapter 2 Calculation of income tax

1

	✓
0%, 20%, 40% and 45%	
40% and 45%	
20% only	
20%, 40% and 45%	✓

2 | £ | 1,265 |

Workings

	Non-savings income £	Savings income £	Dividend income £	Total £
Net income	17,450	2,000	3,000	22,450
Less personal allowance	(12,500)	–	–	(12,500)
Taxable income	4,950	2,000	3,000	9,950

	£
Tax on non-savings income	
4,950 × 20%	990
Tax on savings income	
1,000 × 0%	0
1,000 × 20%	200
Tax on dividend income	
2,000 × 0%	0
1,000 × 7.5%	75
Tax liability	1,265

Albert is a basic rate taxpayer so has a personal savings allowance of £1,000. The dividend allowance is always £2,000.

3 | £ | 67,668 |

Workings

	Non-savings income £	Savings income £	Dividend income £	Total £
Employment income	140,000			140,000
Interest		20,000		20,000
Dividends			30,000	30,000
Net income	140,000	20,000	30,000	190,000
Less personal allowance	(Nil)			(Nil)
Taxable income	140,000	20,000	30,000	190,000

The personal allowance and personal savings allowance are nil because the net income is so high.

	£
Tax on non-savings income	
37,500 × 20%	7,500
102,500 × 40%	41,000
140,000	
Tax on savings income	
10,000 × 40%	4,000
150,000	
10,000 × 45%	4,500
160,000	
Tax on dividend income	
2,000 × 0%	0
28,000 × 38.1%	10,668
190,000	
Income tax liability	67,668

4   Basic rate tax relief is obtained by paying Gift Aid donations net of 20% tax. Further tax relief is given to higher and additional rate taxpayers by extending the basic and higher rate bands by the gross amount of the Gift Aid donation.

5

	Non-savings income £	Savings income £	Dividend income £	Total £
Pension income	17,000			17,000
Property income	4,350			4,350
Interest		380		380
Dividends			700	700
Net income	21,350	380	700	22,430
Less personal allowance	(12,500)			(12,500)
Taxable income	8,850	380	700	9,930

Premium bond prizes are exempt from income tax. She is a basic rate taxpayer so receives the full personal savings allowance of £1,000. The £2,000 dividend allowance is also available.

	£
Tax on non-savings income £8,850 × 20%	1,770
Tax on savings income £380 × 0%	0
Tax on dividend income £700 × 0%	0
	1,770
Less tax deducted from pension income (given)	(1,850)
Income tax repayable	(80)

6

	Non-savings income £	Savings income £	Dividend income £	Total £
Business profits	39,600			39,600
Building society interest		2,000		2,000
Dividends			12,000	12,000
Net income	39,600	2,000	12,000	53,600
Less personal allowance	(12,500)			(12,500)
Taxable income	27,100	2,000	12,000	41,100

Tax on non-savings income	£
£27,100 × 20%	5,420
Tax on savings income	
£500 × 0%	0
£1,500 × 20%	300
Tax on dividend income	
£2,000 × 0%	0
$\dfrac{£8,400}{£39,500} \times 7.5\%$	630

£1,600 × 32.5% (£12,000 – £2,000 – £8,400)	520
Income tax liability/payable	6,870

Note. Gross Gift Aid payment = £1,600 × 100/80 = £2,000. Basic rate extends to £39,500.

Adjusted net income = £53,600 – £2,000 = £51,600 > £50,000 so £500 personal savings allowance available.

7

	✓
£37,500	
£52,500	
£56,250	✓
£62,500	

Workings

£15,000 × 100/80 = £18,750 + £37,500

£37,500 is the basic rate band without the adjustment for gift aid. £52,500 is the basic rate band plus the **net** gift aid payment. £62,500 grosses up the gift aid payment by 100/60.

Chapter 3 Employment income

1 | for services | | of service |

2 | wholly | | exclusively | | necessarily |

3 | £ | (800) |

Workings

	£
Amount received: 8,000 × 35p	2,800
Less statutory limit: 8,000 × 45p	(3,600)
Deductible amount	(800)

4 | £ | 5,900 |

being the higher of the annual value and rent actually paid by the employer.

5

	✓
True	
False	✓

There is a taxable fuel benefit unless the employer is fully reimbursed for private fuel.

6

	✓
£325	
£400	
£175	
£250	✓

Workings

The benefit is the higher of:

		£	£
(a)	Current MV	325	
(b)	Original MV	500	
	Less already assessed (in 2019/20)		
	£500 × 20%	(100)	
		400	
			400
	Less amount paid		(150)
	Taxable benefit		250

£325 uses the current market value without deduction of the amount paid. £400 ignores the amount paid. £175 uses the current market value and deducts the amount paid.

7

	✓
True	
False	✓

Only if total loans do not exceed £10,000 at any time in the tax year are they ignored.

8 | £ | 1,920 |
|---|---|

Workings

Percentage = 6% (from tax tables) + 2% (pre April 2020) = 8%
Benefit 8% × £24,000 = <u>£1,920</u>

9 | £ | 28,950 |
|---|---|

	£
Car benefit (W)	21,600
Fuel benefit (£24,500 × 30%)	7,350
Telephone benefit (exempt – one mobile phone)	Nil
Total benefit	28,950

Workings

CO_2 emissions = 135 g/km (rounded down)

Above baseline: 135 – 55 = 80 g/km
Divide 80 by 5 = 16%
Percentage = 14% + 16% = 30%
£72,000 × 30% = £21,600

10

Item	Taxable	Exempt
Write off loan of £8,000 (only loan provided)	✓	
Payments by employer of £500 per month into registered pension scheme		✓
Provision of one mobile phone		✓
Provision of a company car for both business and private use	✓	
Removal costs of £5,000 paid to an employee relocating to another branch		✓
Accommodation provided to enable the employee to spend longer time in the office	✓	

Chapter 4 Property income

1 | £ | 1,800 |

Rent received 1 December 2020 and 1 March 2021 = $^2/_4 \times £3,600$

2 | £ | 5,200 |

Workings

Insurance premium paid in 2020/21 = payment on 1 October 2020

3 | £ | 6,667 |

Workings

	£
Rental income – first tenants ($£4,000 \times {}^8/_{12}$)	2,667
Rental income – second tenants	5,000
Less expenses	(1,000)
Taxable rental income	6,667

4 To minimise their tax liability the property should be | held in Ben's name |

Polly is paying tax at 45%, Ben is paying tax at 20% so if the asset is held by Polly she will pay tax of £12,000 × 45% = £5,400 whereas if the asset is held by Ben he will pay tax of £12,000 × 20% = £2,400 saving them together £3,000.

5

	✓
Carried back one year and offset against property income only	
Offset against net income in the current year	
Carried forward for one year only and offset against property income	
Carried forward indefinitely and offset against property income only	✓

Chapter 5 National Insurance

1   The Class 1 Employee National Insurance is | £ | 4,3,900 |

The Class 1 Employer National Insurance is | £ | 4,583 |

The Class 1A National Insurance is | £ | 1,104 |

Workings

Class 1 Employee
Robert suffers Class 1 employee contributions on his cash earnings.
There is no National Insurance on his reimbursed expenses.

$(42,000 - 9,500) \times 12\% =$ 3,900

Class 1 Employer
$(42,000 - 8,788) \times 13.8\% =$ 4,583

Class 1A
8,000 @ 13.8% =   1,104

2

Alec's employee contributions are | £ | 3,497 |

Alec's employer contributions are | £ | 5,136 |

Monthly salary 36,000/12 = 3,000
March receipt 3,000 + 10,000 = 13,000

Employee contributions

	£
11 months	
£(3,000 – 792) = £2,208 × 12% × 11 (main only)	2,915
1 month (March)	
£(4,167 – 792) = £3,375 × 12% (main)	405
£(13,000 – 4,167) = £8,833 × 2% (additional)	177
Total employee contributions	3,497

Employer contributions

	£
11 months	
£(3,000 – 732) = £2,268 × 13.8% × 11	3,443
1 month (March)	
£(13,000 – 732) = £12,268 × 13.8%	1,693
Total employer contributions	5,136

3   Elizabeth's employee contributions are   £ | 5,040

Elizabeth's employer contributions are   £ | 6,929

Elizabeth is a director so her National Insurance is calculated on a cumulative basis. This means that the calculation can be done on an annual basis.

Her annual earnings are £49,000 + £10,000 = £59,000

Employee contributions

	£
£(50,000 – 9,500) = £40,500 × 12% (main)	4,860
£(59,000 – 50,000) = £9,000 × 2% (additional)	180
Total employee contributions	5,040

Employer contributions

	£
£(59,000 – 8,788) = £50,212 × 13.8%	6,929

4   The Class 1 employer contributions payable by Ursa Minor Beta plc are

£ | 5,304

	£
Employee 1: £(25,000 – 8,788) = 16,212 × 13.8%	2,237
Employee 2: £(60,000 – 8,788) = 51,212 × 13.8%	7,067
	9,304
Less employment allowance (maximum)	(4,000)
Employer contributions	5,304

5   If the mileage allowance is 35p a mile the amount subject to Class 1 National

Insurance is   £ | nil

If the mileage allowance is 50p a mile the amount subject to Class 1 National

Insurance is   £ | 925

Workings

If the mileage allowance is 35p

	£
Mileage allowance received (18,500 × 35p)	6,475
Permitted payment (18,500 × 45p)	(8,325)
Excess over limit	0

As the payment is within the permitted amount there is no charge to National Insurance.

If the mileage allowance is 50p

	£
Mileage allowance received (18,500 × 50p)	9,250
Less tax-free amount (above)	(8,325)
Excess over limit	925

As the payment is above the permitted amount the excess of £925 will be chargeable to Class 1 National Insurance, employee and employer.

Chapter 6 Chargeable gains

1

	Chargeable ✓	Exempt ✓
A gift of an antique necklace	✓	
The sale of a building	✓	
Sale of a racehorse		✓

2

	£
Proceeds of sale	200,000
Less cost	(80,000)
Less enhancement expenditure	(10,000)
Chargeable gain	110,000

3 £ 143,400

£ 0

	£
Gains	171,000
Less current year losses	(5,300)
	165,700
Less annual exempt amount	(12,300)
	153,400
Less capital losses b/f	(10,000)
Taxable gains	143,400

4 £ 2,500

	£
Chargeable gains	24,800
Less annual exempt amount	(12,300)
Taxable gains	12,500
CGT on £12,500 @ 20%	2,500

5 31/01/2022

6

	✓
£16,663	✓
£17,500	
£19,663	
£18,337	

	£
Proceeds	38,000
Less costs of disposal	(3,000)
	35,000
Less £41,500 × $\frac{38,000}{38,000+48,000}$	(18,337)
Chargeable gain	16,663

£17,500 is the cost from the part disposal calculation using the net proceeds. £19,663 ignores costs of disposal. £18,337 is the cost from the part-disposal calculation.

7

(a)

£	Nil

There is no gain as the chattel cost and gross proceeds are both less than £6,000.

(b)

£	4,033

	£
Gross proceeds	8,420
Less selling expenses	(220)
Net proceeds	8,200
Less cost	(3,500)
	4,700

Gain cannot exceed $^5/_3$ (8,420 – 6,000) = £4,033

Therefore, gain is £4,033

8

	✓
True	
False	✓

A loss on a disposal to a connected person can be set only against gains arising on disposals to the same connected person.

9

	✓
True	✓
False	

10

	Actual proceeds used	Deemed proceeds (market value) used	No gain or loss basis
Paul sells an asset to his civil partner Joe for £3,600.			✓
Grandmother gives an asset to her grandchild worth £1,000.		✓	
Sarah sells an asset worth £20,000 to her best friend Cathy for £12,000. Sarah knows the asset is worth £20,000.		✓*	

*A disposal is deemed to take place at market value when it is deliberately sold for consideration of less than market value.

Chapter 7 Share disposals

1

	✓
£15,750	
£11,500	
£17,000	
£14,250	✓

	No of shares	Cost £
August 1994 acquisition	10,000	5,000
April 2009 acquisition	10,000	16,000
	20,000	21,000
November 2020 disposal	(15,000)	(15,750)
(£21,000 × 15,000/20,000 = £15,750)		
c/f	5,000	5,250

		£
Proceeds of sale		30,000
Less allowable cost		(15,750)
Chargeable gain		14,250

£15,750 is the allowable cost. £11,500 is the gain calculated on a LIFO basis. £17,000 is the gain calculated on a FIFO basis.

2

	✓
True	
False	✓

In a rights issue, shares are paid for and this amount is added to the original cost. In a bonus issue, shares are not paid for and so there is no adjustment to the original cost.

3   £   3,750

	No of shares	Cost £
May 2003 acquisition	2,000	12,000
December 2004 1 for 2 rights issue @ £7.50	1,000	7,500
($^1/_2$ × 2,000 = 1,000 shares × £7.50 = £7,500)		
	3,000	19,500
March 2021 disposal	(2,500)	(16,250)
(£19,500 × 2,500/3,000)		
c/f	500	3,250

		£
Proceeds of sale		20,000
Less allowable costs		(16,250)
Chargeable gain		3,750

4   £   7,000

	No of shares	Cost £
June 2011 acquisition	6,000	15,000
August 2012 1 for 3 bonus issue ($^1/_3$ × 6,000 = 2,000 shares)	2,000	nil
	8,000	15,000
December 2020 disposal (ie all the shares)	(8,000)	(15,000)
c/f	nil	nil

		£
Proceeds of sale		22,000
Less allowable costs		(15,000)
Chargeable gain		7,000

5   The matching rules for shares disposed of are:

   (a)   Shares acquired on the same day
   (b)   Shares acquired in the next 30 days
   (c)   Shares from the share pool

Chapter 8 Private residence relief

1

	✓
6	
9	✓
18	
24	

2 The last nine months of ownership is deemed occupation if, at some time, the residence has been the taxpayer's main residence.

Providing the taxpayer actually occupies the property both at some point before and at some point after the period of absence, the following periods are deemed occupation for the purpose of private residence exemption:

(a) Periods of up to three years for any reason. Where a period of absence exceeds three years, three years out of the longer period are deemed to be a period of occupation.

(b) Periods during which the owner was required by their employment to live abroad.

(c) Period of up to four years where the owner was:

   (i) Self-employed and forced to work away from home (UK and abroad)

   (ii) Employed and required to work elsewhere in the UK (overseas employment is covered by (b) above)

3

	£
Proceeds	180,000
Cost	(60,000)
Gain before private residence exemption	120,000
Private residence exemption 127/212 × £120,000	(71,887)
Chargeable gain	48,113

Workings

Total period of ownership: 1 April 2003 to 30 November 2020 = 17 years and 8 months (212 months)

	Exempt months	Chargeable months
1 April 2003 to 31 July 2006 (actual occupation)	40	
1 August 2006 to 31 July 2010 (employed abroad)	48	
1 August 2010 to 31 January 2013 (actual occupation)	30	
1 February 2013 to 29 February 2020		85
1 March 2020 to 30 November 2020 (last nine months)	9	
	127	85

Exempt 127/212 × £120,000 = <u>£71,887</u>

4

	✓
19.75/25	
14/25	
14.75/25	✓
19/25	

The five years posted abroad will not be deemed occupation as he never returned to live in the property. Therefore, only the actual 14 years of occupation and the last nine months of ownership will be exempt.

19.75 includes the five years posted abroad. 14 ignores the last nine months deemed occupation. 19 includes the five years posted abroad and ignores the last nine months deemed occupation.

5

	✓
True	✓
False	

Clare was in actual occupation from April 2014 to October 2020.

The last nine months of ownership are exempt because Clare had previously lived in the flat as her only or main residence. Therefore, this covers her period of absence from October 2020 to March 2021.

1

	✓
£150,000	✓
£200,000	
£80,000	
£120,000	

	£
Before the gift: 70% shareholding	350,000
After the gift: 50% shareholding	(200,000)
Transfer of value	150,000

£200,000 is the value of her shareholding after the gift. £80,000 is the value of a 20% shareholding from the table. £120,000 is 20% of shares based on the value of a 100% shareholding.

2

	✓
£811,250	
£461,250	
£536,250	
£651,250	✓

	£
Sunita's unused nil rate band £325,000 × 65%	211,250
Joel's nil rate band	325,000
	536,250
Less used against Joel's PET now chargeable	(75,000)
Available nil rate band to set against Joel's death estate	461,250
Residence nil rate band – lower of:	
Value of house left to direct descendants	190,000
Maximum threshold £175,000 × 2	350,000
Available RNRB to set against Joel's death estate	190,000
Total nil rate bands (£461,250 + £190,000)	651,250

£811,250 does not limit the value of the RNRB to the value of the house. £461,250 does not include the RNRB. £536,250 ignores the amount of the NRB used by the PET and ignores the RNRB.

3

	✓
£28,250	
£31,250	
£29,750	✓
£23,800	

	£
Gift	190,000
Less AE × 2 (2020/21 + 2019/20 b/f)	(6,000)
	184,000
Less nil rate band available £(325,000 – 260,000)	(65,000)
	119,000
IHT @ $^{20}/_{80}$	29,750

£28,250 deducts AEs from the value of the historic CLT ie increases the NRB remaining. £31,250 does not deduct the annual exemptions from the value of the gift. £23,800 calculates the tax at 20% instead of 20/80.

4

	✓
£21,000	
Nil	✓
£2,000	
£19,000	

The gift to the granddaughter is covered by the marriage exemption of £2,500 by a remoter ancestor. There was no gratuitous intent on the sale at undervalue of the vase so there is no charge to inheritance tax on this transaction.

5

	✓
£170,000	
£88,000	
£136,000	✓
£132,160	

	£
PET on 10.7.17 PET now chargeable	600,000
Less nil rate band available £(325,000 – 150,000)	(175,000)
	425,000
IHT @ 40%	170,000
Less taper relief (3 to 4 years) @ 20%	(34,000)
Death tax payable on lifetime transfer	136,000

The chargeable lifetime transfer on 15 September 2013 is cumulated with the later PET since it was made in the seven years before that transfer.

£170,000 ignores taper relief. £88,000 deducts the full NRB. £132,160 includes AEs for both the CLT and PET.

6

	✓
£9,350	
£100	
£9,000	
£350	✓

The gifts to the grandson are exempt as normal expenditure out of income because they are part of the normal expenditure of the donor, made out of income and left the donor with sufficient income to maintain her usual standard of living.

The small gifts exemption only applies to gifts up to £250 per donee per tax year. If gifts total more than £250 the whole amount is chargeable. Since the gifts to the grand-nephew totalled £(100 + 250) = £350 in 2020/21, this exemption does not apply.

7

	✓
£60,000	
£27,000	
£66,000	✓
£84,000	

	£
Before the gift: 100% shareholding 1,000 × £150	150,000
After the gift: 70% shareholding 700 × £120	(84,000)
Transfer of value	66,000

£60,000 is the diminution in value less annual exemptions. £27,000 is the value of 30% shareholding. £84,000 is the value of Daniel's shares after the gift

8 | £ | 24,000 |

	£
House (net of mortgage) £(200,000 – 60,000)	140,000
Investments and cash	350,000
	490,000
Less funeral expenses	(5,000)
	485,000
Less exempt gift to spouse	(100,000)
Chargeable death estate	385,000
Less available nil rate band (no lifetime transfers)	(325,000)
	60,000
IHT @ 40%	24,000

Note. there is no RNRB as the property was an investment rather than Susanna's home.

9 | £ | 351,000 |

	£
Cash to nephews £200 × 5	1,000
ISA investments	350,000
Balance of estate	520,000
Exempt transfer to spouse	(520,000)
Chargeable estate	351,000

The small gifts exemption only applies to lifetime transfers. The ISA exemption only applies for income tax and capital gains tax. The residue to the wife is covered by the spouse exemption.

Lifetime tax	Death tax	✓
Ruth	Ruth's estate	
Ruth	Trustees	✓
Trustees	Ruth's estate	
Trustees	Trustees	

The tax rate of $^{20}/_{80}$ shows that Ruth paid the tax on the lifetime transfer. The recipient always pays the death tax on the lifetime gift.

Chapter 10 The tax and ethical framework

1

	True ✓	False ✓
All taxpayers are sent a tax return each year by HM Revenue & Customs.		✓

Most taxpayers are employees who have their tax deducted at source under PAYE so they do not need to complete a tax return.

2

	✓
The Chancellor of the Exchequer	
Companies House	
HM Revenue & Customs	✓
Members of Parliament	

3

	✓
Acts of Parliament	✓
HMRC statements of practice	
Statutory instruments	✓
Extra statutory concessions	

4

	✓
When in a social environment	
When discussing client affairs with third parties with the client's proper and specific authority	✓
When reading documents relating to the client's affairs in public places	
When preparing tax returns	

5

	✓
HMRC	
Nearest police station	
National Crime Agency	✓
Tax tribunal	

6   You should tell Cornelius that under the AAT guidelines on client confidentiality, you cannot provide him with any information on another client without the specific authority of that client.

7

	✓
Tax planning	✓
Tax avoidance	
Tax evasion	
Not possible to say until decided by a judge	

8

	✓
Progressive	
Regressive	
Proportional	✓
Equitable	

9

	✓
Not resident or domiciled	
Not resident but domiciled	✓
Resident but not domiciled	
Resident and domiciled	

By leaving the UK he has lost his residence status. He will only lose his domicile status if he takes active steps to show he plans to never return to the UK.

10

	✓
Taxed on all of his income in the UK regardless as to where it is earned	
Taxed in the UK on his UK income and income brought into the UK from overseas	
Taxed in the UK only on his UK income	✓
Not taxed in the UK	

Pierre is not in the UK long enough to be resident. He has never come to the UK before so he cannot be domiciled. He will therefore only be taxed on UK income, for example, the interest earned on his UK bank account.

Tax tables 2020/21

1 Tax rates and bands

Tax rates	Tax bands	Normal rates %	Dividend rates %
Basic rate	£1–£37,500	20	7.5
Higher rate	£37,501–£150,000	40	32.5
Additional rate	£150,001 and over	45	38.1

2 Allowances

		£
Personal allowance		12,500
Savings allowance:	Basic rate taxpayer	1,000
	Higher rate taxpayer	500
Dividend allowance		2,000
Income limit for personal allowances*		100,000

*Personal allowances are reduced by £1 for every £2 over the income limit.

3 Property income allowance

	£
Annual limit	1,000

4 Individual savings accounts

	£
Annual limit	20,000

5 Car benefit percentage

CO_2 Emissions for petrol engines g/km	Electric range miles	Cars first registered from 6 April 2020 %
Nil		0
1 to 50	130 or more	0
1 to 50	70-129	3
1 to 50	40-69	6
1 to 50	30-39	10
1 to 50	Less than 30	12
51 to 54		13
55 or more		14 + 1% for every extra 5g/km above 55g/km
Registration pre 6 April 2020*		Additional 2%
Diesel engines**		Additional 4%

* The additional 2% does not apply to pure electric vehicles

** The additional 4% will not apply to diesel cars which are registered after 1 September 2017 and they meet the RDE2 standards.

6 Car fuel benefit

	£
Base figure	24,500

7 Approved mileage allowance payments (employees and residential landlords)

First 10,000 miles	45p per mile
Over 10,000 miles	25p per mile
Additional passengers	5p per mile per passenger
Motorcycles	24p per mile
Bicycles	20p per mile

8 Van benefit charge

	£
Basic charge	3,490
Private fuel charge	666
	%
Benefit charge for zero emission vans	80

9 Other benefits in kind

Expensive accommodation limit	£75,000
Health screening	One per year
Incidental overnight expenses: within UK	£5 per night
Incidental overnight expenses: overseas	£10 per night
Job-related accommodation	£Nil
Living expenses where job-related exemption applies	Restricted to 10% of employees net earnings
Loan of assets annual charge	20%
Low-rate or interest free loans	Up to £10,000
Mobile telephones	One per employee
Non-cash gifts from someone other than the employer	£250 per tax year
Non-cash long service award	£50 per year of service
Pay whilst attending a full time course	£15,480 per academic year
Provision of eye tests and spectacles for VDU use	£Nil
Provision of parking spaces	£Nil
Provision of workplace childcare	£Nil
Provision of workplace sports facilities	£Nil
Removal and relocation expenses	£8,000
Staff party or event	£150 per head
Staff suggestion scheme	Up to £5,000
Subsidised meals	£Nil
Working from home	£6 per week / £26 per month

10 HMRC official rate

HMRC official rate	2.25%

11 National insurance contributions

		%
Class 1 Employee:	Below £9,500	0
	Above £9,500 and Below £50,000	12
	£50,000 and above	2
Class 1 Employer:	Below £8,788	0
	£8,788 and above	13.8
Class 1A		13.8
		£
Employment allowance		4,000

12 Capital gains tax

	£
Annual exempt amount	12,300

13 Capital gains tax - tax rates

	%
Basic rate	10
Higher rate	20

14 Inheritance tax – tax rates

		£
Nil rate band		325,000
Additional residence nil-rate band*		175,000
		%
Excess taxable at:	Death rate	40
	Lifetime rate	20

* Applies when a home is passed on death to direct descendants of the deceased after 6 April 2017. Any unused band is transferrable to a spouse or civil partner.

15 Inheritance tax – tapering relief

	% reduction
3 years or less	0
Over 3 years but less than 4 years	20
Over 4 years but less than 5 years	40
Over 5 years but less than 6 years	60
Over 6 years but less than 7 years	80

16 Inheritance – exemptions

		£
Small gifts		250 per transferee per tax year
Marriage or civil partnership:	From parent	5,000
	Grandparent	2,500
	One party to the other	2,500
	Others	1,000
Annual exemption		3,000

17 Deemed domicile

Deemed domicile	Criteria
Condition A	Was born in the UK
	Domicile of origin was in the UK
	Was resident in the UK for 2017 to 2018 or later years
Condition B	Has been UK resident for at least 15 of the 20 tax years immediately before the relevant tax year

Reference material

1 Interpretation and abbreviations

Context

Tax advisors operate in a complex business and financial environment. The increasing public focus on the role of taxation in wider society means a greater interest in the actions of tax advisors and their clients.

This guidance, written by the professional bodies for their members working in tax, sets out the hallmarks of a good tax advisor, and in particular the fundamental principles of behaviour that members are expected to follow.

Interpretation

1.1   In this guidance:

- 'Client' includes, where the context requires, 'former client'.

- 'Member' (and 'members') includes 'firm' or 'practice' and the staff thereof.

- Words in the singular include the plural and words in the plural include the singular.

Abbreviations

1.2   The following abbreviations have been used:

AML	Anti-Money Laundering
CCAB	Consultative Committee of Accountancy Bodies
DOTAS	Disclosure of Tax Avoidance Schemes
GAAP	Generally Accepted Accounting Principles
GAAR	General Anti-Abuse Rule in Finance Act 2013
GDPR	General Data Protection Regulation
HMRC	Her Majesty's Revenue and Customs
MTD	Making Tax Digital
MLRO	Money Laundering Reporting Officer
NCA	National Crime Agency (previously the Serious Organised Crime Agency, SOCA)
POTAS	Promoters of Tax Avoidance Schemes
PCRT	Professional Conduct in Relation to Taxation
SRN	Scheme Reference Number

2 Fundamental principles

Overview of the fundamental principles

2.1 Ethical behaviour in the tax profession is critical. The work carried out by a member needs to be trusted by society at large as well as by clients and other stakeholders. What a member does reflects not just on themselves but on the profession as a whole.

2.2 A member must comply with the following fundamental principles:

Integrity

To be straightforward and honest in all professional and business relationships.

Objectivity

To not allow bias, conflict of interest or undue influence of others to override professional or business judgements.

Professional competence and due care

To maintain professional knowledge and skill at the level required to ensure that a client or employer receives competent professional service based on current developments in practice, legislation and techniques and act diligently and in accordance with applicable technical and professional standards.

Confidentiality

To respect the confidentiality of information acquired as a result of professional and business relationships and, therefore, not disclose any such information to third parties without proper and specific authority, unless there is a legal or professional right or duty to disclose, nor use the information for the personal advantage of the member or third parties.

Professional behaviour

To comply with relevant laws and regulations and avoid any action that discredits the profession.

3 PCRT Help sheet A: Submission of tax information and 'Tax filings'

Definition of filing of tax information and tax filings (filing)

3.1 For the purposes of this guidance, the term 'filing' includes any online submission of data, online filing or other filing that is prepared on behalf of the client for the purposes of disclosing to any taxing authority details that are to be used in the calculation of tax due by a client or a refund of tax due to the client or for other official purposes. It includes all taxes, NIC and duties.

3.2 A letter, or online notification, giving details in respect of a filing or as an amendment to a filing including, for example, any voluntary disclosure of an error should be dealt with as if it was a filing.

Making Tax Digital and filing

3.3 Tax administration systems, including the UK's, are increasingly moving to mandatory digital filing of tax information and returns.

3.4 Except in exceptional circumstances, a member will explicitly file in their capacity as agent. A member is advised to use the facilities provided for agents and to avoid knowing or using the client's personal access credentials.

3.5 A member should keep their access credentials safe from unauthorised use and consider periodic change of passwords.

3.6 A member is recommended to forward suspicious emails to phishing@hmrc.gsi.gov.uk and then delete them. It is also important to avoid clicking on websites or links in suspicious emails, or opening attachments.

3.7 Firms should have policies on cyber security, AML and GDPR.

Taxpayer's responsibility

3.8 The taxpayer has primary responsibility to submit correct and complete filings to the best of their knowledge and belief. The final decision as to whether to disclose any issue is that of the client but in relation to your responsibilities see paragraph 12 below.

3.9 In annual self-assessment returns or returns with short filing periods the filing may include reasonable estimates where necessary.

Member's responsibility

3.10 A member who prepares a filing on behalf of a client is responsible to the client for the accuracy of the filing based on the information provided.

3.11 In dealing with HMRC in relation to a client's tax affairs a member should bear in mind their duty of confidentiality to the client and that they are acting as the agent of their client. They have a duty to act in the best interests of their client.

3.12 A member should act in good faith in dealings with HMRC in accordance with the fundamental principle of integrity. In particular the member should take reasonable care and exercise appropriate professional scepticism when making statements or asserting facts on behalf of a client.

3.13 Where acting as a tax agent, a member is not required to audit the figures in the books and records provided or verify information provided by a client or by a third party. However, a member should take care not to be associated with the presentation of facts they know or believe to be incorrect or misleading, not to assert tax positions in a tax filing which they consider to have no sustainable basis.

3.14 When a member is communicating with HMRC, they should consider whether they need to make it clear to what extent they are relying on information which has been supplied by the client or a third party.

Materiality

3.15 Whether an amount is to be regarded as material depends upon the facts and circumstances of each case.

3.16 The profits of a trade, profession, vocation or property business should be computed in accordance with GAAP subject to any adjustment required or authorised by law in computing profits for those purposes. This permits a trade, profession, vocation or property business to disregard non-material adjustments in computing its accounting profits.

3.17 The application of GAAP, and therefore materiality does not extend beyond the accounting profits. Thus, the accounting concept of materiality cannot be applied when completing tax filings.

3.18 It should be noted that for certain small businesses an election may be made to use the cash basis instead; for small property businesses the default position is the cash basis. Where the cash basis is used, materiality is not relevant.

Disclosure

3.19 If a client is unwilling to include in a tax filing the minimum information required by law, the member should follow the guidance in Help sheet C: Dealing with Errors. The paragraphs below (paras 20 – 24) give guidance on some of the more common areas of uncertainty over disclosure.

3.20 In general, it is likely to be in a client's own interests to ensure that factors relevant to their tax liability are adequately disclosed to HMRC because:

- their relationship with HMRC is more likely to be on a satisfactory footing if they can demonstrate good faith in their dealings with them. HMRC notes in 'Your Charter' that 'We want to give you a service that is fair, accurate and based on mutual trust and respect'

- they will reduce the risk of a discovery or further assessment and may reduce exposure to interest and penalties.

3.21 It may be advisable to consider fuller disclosure than is strictly necessary. Reference to 'The Standards for Tax Planning' in PCRT may be relevant. The factors involved in making this decision include:

- a filing relies on a valuation
- the terms of the applicable law
- the view taken by the member
- the extent of any doubt that exists
- the manner in which disclosure is to be made
- the size and gravity of the item in question.

3.22 When advocating fuller disclosure than is necessary a member should ensure that their client is adequately aware of the issues involved and their potential implications. Fuller disclosure should only be made with the client's consent.

3.23 Cases will arise where there is doubt as to the correct treatment of an item of income or expenditure, or the computation of a gain or allowance. In such cases a member ought to consider what additional disclosure, if any, might be necessary. For example, additional disclosure should be considered where:

- there is inherent doubt as to the correct treatment of an item, for example, expenditure on repairs which might be regarded as capital in whole or part, or the VAT liability of a particular transaction, or

- HMRC has published its interpretation or has indicated its practice on a point, but the client proposes to adopt a different view, whether or not supported by Counsel's opinion. The member should refer to the guidance on the Veltema case and the paragraph below. See also HMRC guidance.

3.24 A member who is uncertain whether their client should disclose a particular item or of its treatment should consider taking further advice before reaching a decision. They should use their best endeavours to ensure that the client understands the issues, implications and the proposed course of action. Such a decision may have to be justified at a later date, so the member's files should contain sufficient evidence to support the position taken, including timely notes of discussions with the client and/or with other advisors, copies of any second opinion obtained and the client's final decision. A failure to take reasonable care may result in HMRC imposing a penalty if an error is identified after an enquiry.

Supporting documents

3.25 For the most part, HMRC does not consider that it is necessary for a taxpayer to provide supporting documentation in order to satisfy the taxpayer's overriding need to make a correct filing. HMRC's view is that, where it is necessary for that purpose, explanatory information should be entered in the 'white space' provided on the filing. However, HMRC does recognise that the taxpayer may wish to supply further details of a particular computation or transaction in order to minimise the risk of a discovery assessment being raised at a later time. Following the uncertainty created by the decision in Veltema, HMRC's guidance can be found in SP1/06 – Self Assessment: Finality and Discovery.

3.26 Further HMRC guidance says that sending attachments with a tax filing is intended for those cases where the taxpayer 'feels it is crucial to provide additional information to support the filing but for some reason cannot utilise the white space'.

Reliance on HMRC published guidance

3.27 Whilst it is reasonable in most circumstances to rely on HMRC published guidance, a member should be aware that the Tribunal and the courts will apply the law even if this conflicts with HMRC guidance.

3.28 Notwithstanding this, if a client has relied on HMRC guidance which is clear and unequivocal and HMRC resiles from any of the terms of the guidance, a Judicial Review claim is a possible route to pursue.

Approval of tax filings

3.29 The member should advise the client to review their tax filing before it is submitted.

3.30 The member should draw the client's attention to the responsibility which the client is taking in approving the filing as correct and complete. Attention should be drawn to any judgmental areas or positions reflected in the filing to ensure that the client is aware of these and their implications before they approve the filing.

3.31 A member should obtain evidence of the client's approval of the filing in electronic or non-electronic form.

4 PCRT Help sheet B: Tax advice

The Standards for Tax Planning

4.1 The Standards for Tax Planning are critical to any planning undertaken by members. They are:

- Client Specific

  Tax planning must be specific to the particular client's facts and circumstances. Clients must be alerted to the wider risks and implications of any courses of action.

- Lawful

  At all times members must act lawfully and with integrity and expect the same from their clients. Tax planning should be based on a realistic assessment of the facts and on a credible view of the law.

  Members should draw their client's attention to where the law is materially uncertain, for example because HMRC is known to take a different view of the law. Members should consider taking further advice appropriate to the risks and circumstances of the particular case, for example where litigation is likely.

- Disclosure and transparency

  Tax advice must not rely for its effectiveness on HMRC having less than the relevant facts. Any disclosure must fairly represent all relevant facts.

- Tax planning arrangements

  Members must not create, encourage or promote tax planning arrangements or structures that i) set out to achieve results that are contrary to the clear intention of Parliament in enacting relevant legislation and/or ii) are highly artificial or highly contrived and seek to exploit shortcomings within the relevant legislation.

- Professional judgement and appropriate documentation

- Applying these requirements to particular client advisory situations requires members to exercise professional judgement on a number of matters. Members should keep notes on a timely basis of the rationale for the judgements exercised in seeking to adhere to these requirements

Guidance

4.2 The paragraphs below provide guidance for members when considering whether advice complies with the Fundamental Principles and Standards for Tax Planning.

Tax evasion

4.3 A member should never be knowingly involved in tax evasion, although, of course, it is appropriate to act for a client who is rectifying their affairs.

Tax planning and advice

4.4 In contrast to tax evasion, tax planning is legal. However, under the Standard members 'must not create, encourage or promote tax planning arrangements that (i) set out to achieve results that are contrary to the clear intention of Parliament in enacting relevant legislation and/or (ii) are highly artificial or highly contrived and seek to exploit shortcomings within the relevant legislation'.

4.5 Things to consider:

- Have you checked that your engagement letter fully covers the scope of the planning advice?

- Have you taken the Standards for Tax Planning and the Fundamental Principles into account? Is it client specific? Is it lawful? Will all relevant facts be disclosed to HMRC? Is it creating, encouraging or promoting tax planning contrary to the 4th Standard for Tax Planning.

- How tax sophisticated is the client?

- Has the client made clear what they wish to achieve by the planning?

- What are the issues involved with the implementation of the planning?

- What are the risks associated with the planning and have you warned the client of the them? For example:

    - The strength of the legal interpretation relied upon.

    - The potential application of the GAAR.

    - The implications for the client, including the obligations of the client in relation to their tax return, if the planning requires disclosure under DOTAS or DASVOIT and the potential for an accelerated payment notice or partner payment notice?

    - The reputational risk to the client and the member of the planning in the public arena.

    - The stress, cost and wider personal or business implications to the client in the event of a prolonged dispute with HMRC. This may involve unwelcomed publicity, costs, expenses and loss of management time over a significant period.

    - If the client tenders for government contracts, the potential impact of the proposed tax planning on tendering for and retaining public sector contracts.

    - The risk of counteraction. This may occur before the planning is completed or potentially there may be retrospective counteraction at a later date.

- The risk of challenge by HMRC. Such challenge may relate to the legal interpretation relied upon, but may alternatively relate to the construction of the facts, including the implementation of the planning.

- The risk and inherent uncertainty of litigation. The probability of the planning being overturned by the courts if litigated and the potential ultimate downside should the client be unsuccessful.

- Is a second opinion necessary/advisable?

- Are the arrangements in line with any applicable code of conduct or ethical guidelines or stances for example the Banking Code, and fit and proper tests for charity trustees and pension administrators?

- Are you satisfied that the client understands the planning proposed?

- Have you documented the advice given and the reasoning behind it?

5 PCRT Help sheet C: Dealing with errors

Introduction

5.1 For the purposes of this guidance, the term 'error' is intended to include all errors and mistakes whether they were made by the client, the member, HMRC or any other party involved in a client's tax affairs, and whether made innocently or deliberately.

5.2 During a member's relationship with the client, the member may become aware of possible errors in the client's tax affairs. Unless the client is already aware of the possible error, they should be informed as soon as the member identifies them.

5.3 Where the error has resulted in the client paying too much tax the member should advise the client to make a repayment claim. The member should advise the client of the time limits to make a claim and have regard to any relevant time limits. The rest of this Help sheet deals with situations where tax may be due to HMRC.

5.4 Sometimes an error made by HMRC may mean that the client has not paid tax actually due or they have been incorrectly repaid tax. There may be fee costs as a result of correcting such mistakes. A member should bear in mind that, in some circumstances, clients or agents may be able to claim for additional professional costs incurred and compensation from HMRC.

5.5 A member should act correctly from the outset. A member should keep sufficient appropriate records of discussions and advice and when dealing with errors the member should:

- give the client appropriate advice';

- if necessary, so long as they continue to act for the client, seek to persuade the client to behave correctly;

- take care not to appear to be assisting a client to plan or commit any criminal offence or to conceal any offence which has been committed; and

- in appropriate situations, or where in doubt, discuss the client's situation with a colleague or an independent third party (having due regard to client confidentiality).

5.6 Once aware of a possible error, a member must bear in mind the legislation on money laundering and the obligations and duties which this places upon them.

5.7 Where the member may have made the error, the member should consider whether they need to notify their professional indemnity insurers.

5.8 In any situation where a member has concerns about their own position, they should consider taking specialist legal advice. For example, where a client appears to have used the member to assist in the commissioning of a criminal offence and people could question whether the member had acted honestly in in good faith. Note that The Criminal Finances Act 2017 has created new criminal offences of failure to prevent facilitation of tax evasion.

5.9 The flowchart below summarises the recommended steps a member should take where a possible error arises. It must be read in conjunction with the guidance and commentary that follow it.

Dealing with errors flowchart

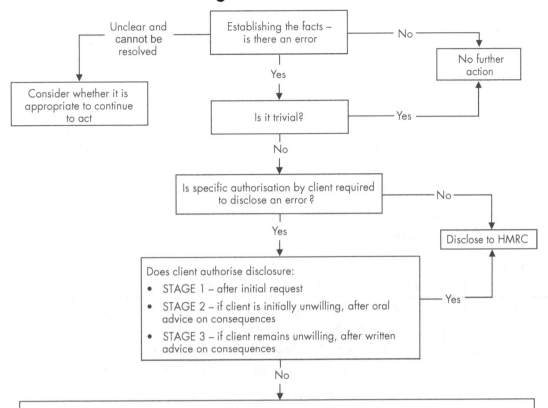

YOU MUST CEASE TO ACT

- Advise client in writing that you no longer act for them in respect of any tax matters and, if relevant, any other client matters.
- Notify HMRC that you have ceased to act, if relevant.
- Consider if you need to advise HMRC that any accounts/statements carrying a report signed by you can no longer be relied upon.
- Consider whether a report should be made to MLRO/NCA.
- Carefully consider your response to any professional enquiry letter.

At all times consider your obligations under anti-money laundering legislation and whether you need to submit a Suspicious Activity Report.

6 PCRT Help sheet D: Requests for data by HMRC

Introduction

6.1 For the purposes of this help sheet the term 'data' includes documents in whatever form (including electronic) and other information. While this guidance relates to HMRC requests, other government bodies or organisations may also approach the member for data. The same principles apply.

6.2 A distinction should be drawn between a request for data made informally ('informal requests') and those requests for data which are made in exercise of a power to require the provision of the data requested ('formal requests').

6.3 Similarly, requests addressed to a client and those addressed to a member require different handling.

6.4 Where a member no longer acts for a client, the member remains subject to the duty of confidentiality. In relation to informal requests, the member should refer the enquirer either to the former client or if authorised by the client to the new agent. In relation to formal requests addressed to the member, the termination of their professional relationship with the client does not affect the member's duty to comply with that request, where legally required to do so.

6.5 A member should comply with formal requests and should not seek to frustrate legitimate requests for information. Adopting a constructive approach may help to resolve issues promptly and minimise costs to all parties.

6.6 Whilst a member should be aware of HMRC's powers it may be appropriate to take specialist advice.

6.7 Devolved tax authorities have separate powers.

6.8 Two flowcharts are at the end of this help sheet;

- Requests for data addressed to the member, and
- Requests for data addressed to the client.

Informal requests addressed to the client

6.9 From time to time HMRC chooses to communicate directly with clients rather than with the appointed agent.

6.10 HMRC has given reassurances that it is working to ensure that initial contact on compliance checks will normally be via the agent and only if the agent does not reply within an appropriate timescale will the contact be directly with the client.

6.11 When the member assists a client in dealing with such requests from HMRC, the member should advise the client that cooperation with informal requests can provide greater opportunities for the taxpayer to find a pragmatic way to work through the issue at hand with HMRC.

Informal requests addressed to the member

6.12 Disclosure in response to informal requests can only be made with the client's permission.

6.13 In many instances, the client will have authorised routine disclosure of relevant data, for example, through the engagement letter. However, if there is any doubt about whether the client has authorised disclosure, the member should ask the client to approve what is to be disclosed.

6.14 Where an oral enquiry is made by HMRC, a member should consider asking for it to be put in writing so that a response may be agreed with the client.

6.15 Although there is no obligation to comply with an informal request in whole or in part, a member should advise the client whether it is in the client's best interests to disclose such data, as lack of cooperation may have a direct impact on penalty negotiations post—enquiry.

6.16 Informal requests may be forerunners to formal requests compelling the disclosure of data. Consequently, it may be sensible to comply with such requests.

Formal requests addressed to the client

6.17 In advising their client a member should consider whether specialist advice may be needed, for example on such issues as whether the notice has been issued in accordance with the relevant tax legislation and whether the data request is valid.

6.18 The member should also advise the client about any relevant right of appeal against the formal request if appropriate and of the consequences of a failure to comply.

6.19 If the notice is legally effective the client is legally obliged to comply with the request.

6.20 The most common statutory notice issued to clients and third parties by HMRC is under Schedule 36 FA 2008.

Formal requests addressed to the member

6.21 The same principles apply to formal requests to the member as formal requests to clients.

6.22 If a formal request is valid it **overrides the member's duty of confidentiality** to their client. The member is therefore obliged to comply with the request. Failure to comply with their legal obligations can expose the member to civil or criminal penalties.

6.23 In cases where the member is not legally precluded by the terms of the notice from communicating with the client, the member should advise the client of the notice and keep the client informed of progress and developments.

6.24 The member should ensure that in complying with any notice they do not provide information or data outside the scope of the notice.

6.25 If a member is faced with a situation in which HMRC is seeking to enforce disclosure by the removal of data, or seeking entrance to inspect business premises occupied by a member in their capacity as an adviser, the member should consider seeking immediate professional advice, to ensure that this is the legally correct course of action.

Privileged data

6.26 Legal privilege arises under common law and may only be overridden if this is set out in legislation. It protects a party's right to communicate in confidence with a legal adviser. The privilege belongs to the client and not to the member.

6.27 If a document is privileged: The client cannot be required to make disclosure of that document to HMRC. Another party cannot disclose it (including the member), without the client's express permission.

6.28 There are two types of legal privilege under common law: legal advice privilege and litigation privilege.

(a) **Legal advice privilege**

Covers documents passing between a client and their legal adviser prepared for the purposes of obtaining or giving legal advice. However, communications from a tax adviser who is not a practising lawyer will not attract legal advice privilege even if such individuals are giving advice on legal matters such as tax law.

(b) **Litigation privilege**

Covers data created for the dominant purpose of litigation. Litigation privilege may arise where litigation has not begun, but is merely contemplated and may apply to data prepared by non-lawyer advisors (including tax advisors). There are two important limits on litigation privilege. First, it does not arise in respect of non-adversarial proceedings. Second, the documents must be produced for the 'dominant purpose' of litigation.

6.29 A privilege under Schedule 36 paragraphs 19, (documents relating to the conduct of a pending appeal), 24 and 25 (auditors, and tax advisors' documents) might exist by "quasi-privilege" and if this is the case a tax adviser does not have to provide those documents. Care should be taken as not all data may be privileged.

6.30 A member who receives a request for data, some of which the member believes may be subject to privilege or 'quasi-privilege', should take independent legal advice on the position, unless expert in this area.

Helpsheet D: Flowchart regarding requests for data by HMRC to the Member

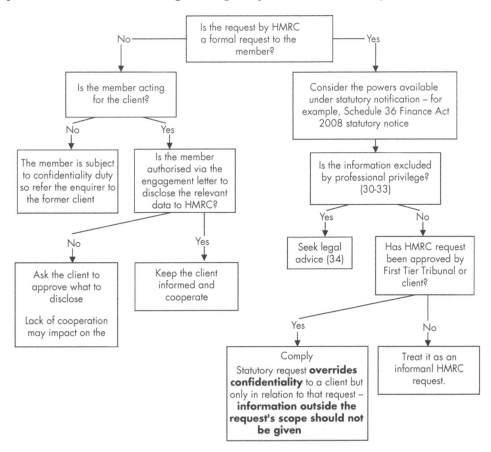

Helpsheet D: Flowchart regarding requests for data by HMRC to the Client

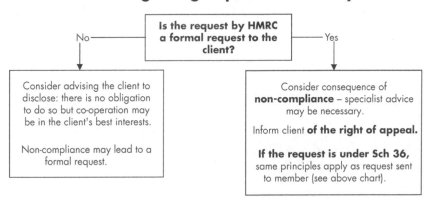

The Reference Materials have been produced by the AAT.

Bibliography

Association of Accounting Technicians (2017) *AAT Code of Professional Ethics.* [Online.] Available from: www.aat.org.uk/prod/s3fs-public/assets/AAT-Code-Professional-Ethics.pdf [Accessed 29 May 2020].

Her Majesty's Revenue and Customs (2019) *Expenses & benefits: A tax guide.* [Online]. Available from: https://assets.publishing.service.gov.uk/government/uploads/system/uploads/attachment_data/file/785476/480_2019_Expenses_benefits.pdf.pdf [Accessed 29 May 2020].

Contains public sector information licensed under the Open Government Licence v3.0.
www.nationalarchives.gov.uk/doc/open-government-licence/version/3/.

Index

REVIEW FORM

How have you used this Course Book?
(Tick one box only)

☐ Self study

☐ On a course_____

☐ Other _____

Why did you decide to purchase this Course Book? *(Tick one box only)*

☐ Have used BPP materials in the past

☐ Recommendation by friend/colleague

☐ Recommendation by a college lecturer

☐ Saw advertising

☐ Other _____

During the past six months do you recall seeing/receiving either of the following?
(Tick as many boxes as are relevant)

☐ Our advertisement in Accounting Technician

☐ Our Publishing Catalogue

Which (if any) aspects of our advertising do you think are useful?
(Tick as many boxes as are relevant)

☐ Prices and publication dates of new editions

☐ Information on Course Book content

☐ Details of our free online offering

☐ None of the above

Your ratings, comments and suggestions would be appreciated on the following areas of this Course Book.

	Very useful	Useful	Not useful
Chapter overviews	☐	☐	☐
Introductory section	☐	☐	☐
Quality of explanations	☐	☐	☐
Illustrations	☐	☐	☐
Chapter activities	☐	☐	☐
Test your learning	☐	☐	☐
Keywords	☐	☐	☐

	Excellent	Good	Adequate	Poor
Overall opinion of this Course Book	☐	☐	☐	☐

Do you intend to continue using BPP Products? ☐ Yes ☐ No

The BPP author of this edition can be emailed at: learningmedia@bpp.com

REVIEW FORM (continued)

TELL US WHAT YOU THINK

Please note any further comments and suggestions/errors below